ROGER MOORE AS JAMES BOND

Roger Moore was born the son of a London policeman in 1927, and was educated mainly at Amersham, where he was evacuated during the war. After school he worked in a film company, and then as an extra on *Caesar and Cleopatra*, where he was 'discovered' by a co-director of the film, Brian Desmond Hurst, who sent him to RADA. After a very happy time there he was conscripted and sent to Germany, Italy and Austria. A period of virtual unemployment followed, until his first big break, when he understudied David Tomlinson in *The Little Hut* with Robert Morley on the London stage. He then went to America where he made films and plays for television and several films for MGM. Disliking the idea of being type-cast, he returned to Europe and made a couple more films until *The Saint* was offered. For seven years he worked on *The Saint*, which was sold to eighty countries and is still being shown. And, although he swore not to do another series, this was followed by the highly successful *The Persuaders!* with Tony Curtis. He lives in Denham with his two children and his Italian wife, Luisa, who took some of the photographs for *Roger Moore as James Bond*.

ROGER MOORE
AS JAMES BOND

Roger Moore's own account of filming
Live and Let Die

With exclusive colour photographs by Luisa Moore
and stills from the film

A Pan Original

PAN BOOKS LTD : LONDON

First published 1973 by Pan Books Ltd,
33 Tothill Street, London SW1

ISBN 0 330 23653 9

Made and printed in Great Britain by
Cox & Wyman Ltd, London, Reading and Fakenham

ACKNOWLEDGEMENTS

I would like to thank Harry Saltzman, Cubby Broccoli, Guy Hamilton, Dan and Hazel Slater and Derek Coyte, without whom this would not have been possible.

I would also like to thank Sean Connery – *with* whom it would not have been possible.

LIST OF ILLUSTRATIONS

between pages 96 and 97

Photographs 2, 3, 5, 6, 7, 9, 10 and 12 were taken exclusively for this book by Luisa Moore. The remainder, and the cover photographs, are by George Whitear, reproduced by kind permission of Eon Productions Ltd

CAST

JAMES BOND	*Roger Moore*
MR BIG	*Yaphet Kotto*
SOLITAIRE	*Jane Seymour*
SHERIFF PEPPER	*Clifton James*
TEE HEE	*Julius W. Harris*
BARON SAMEDI	*Geoffrey Holder*
LEITER	*David Hedison*
ROSIE	*Gloria Hendry*
'M'	*Bernard Lee*
MONEYPENNY	*Lois Maxwell*
ADAM	*Tommy Lane*
WHISPER	*Earl Jolly Brown*
QUARREL	*Roy Stewart*
STRUTTER	*Lon Satton*
CAB DRIVER 1	*Arnold Williams*
MRS BELL	*Ruth Kempf*
CHARLIE	*Joie Chitwood*
BEAUTIFUL GIRL	*Madeline Smith*
DAMBALA	*Michael Ebbin*
SALES GIRL	*Kubi Chaza*
SINGER	*B. J. Arnau*

They say when death is imminent your entire life flashes in front of your eyes. The only thing flashing before my eyes was a large corrugated iron shed sticking up out of the Louisiana bayou which I was approaching at a fair old sixty miles an hour in an out of control boat. I knew I was going to hit it and there was nothing I could do about it. I wound up in a heap on the floor, clutching my mouth, my knee throbbing, my shoulder numb and what felt like fifty-four thousand teeth in my mouth all at once being slowly mangled up into little bits of gravel. The only thing flashing before my eyes was that here I was just about to start playing Bond with no teeth. How on earth did I get myself into such a situation?

It began on Sunday, 8 October 1972, when, as the new James Bond, I left England in a blaze of publicity for the first location in New Orleans. We flew via New York and the journey was hysterical. Danny Kaye was aboard and he started in on the stewardesses straight away. While the girl was standing up in front of the jumbo jet trying to show everybody how to put on a life jacket, there was Danny sitting there miming exactly what the poor girl was doing.

Our arrival in New York, where an elegant suite at the Sherry-Netherland awaited us, was – what can one say? – it was Bond-style. We had two cars laid on to meet us – one for our baggage and one for us. Danny rode in with us and all he wanted to do was stop at a Sixth Avenue delicatessen and pick up some salt beef sandwiches. I wanted to get to the hotel as I was absolutely bushed. When we got to the Sherry-Netherland, where Danny keeps a permanent suite, he spent an hour on the phone trying to find the number of the Sixth Avenue delicatessen. He got them finally, only to discover they weren't prepared to deliver at that hour.

Early next morning Arthur McGhee, the American costume consultant, took me out shopping to find some casual outfits for the film. It was Columbus Day, rather apt for me as Columbus was a man who didn't know where he was going and when he got there he didn't know where he was. All we did was dodge the Columbus Day parades.

Danny took us to Brownies, a health food restaurant on Seventeenth Street, where we were joined by Topol and a very mysterious Israeli gentleman whose name was only mumbled in introduction. I found out afterwards he was the head of the Israeli Air Force who was in America incognito. We were joined there by Arthur, triumphantly toting a dirty-brown Levi suit sixteen sizes too large which he said would boil down to my size.

New Orleans, they say, is different. We arrived. We agreed – it is. My wife Luisa and I felt it straight away. It is a different scene and it is even a different kind of heat. We are staying at a beautiful hotel in the French Quarter called, appropriately enough, the 'French Quarter Inn'.

Wednesday morning began with a rehearsal on the Irish Bayou for the fifteen minute chase sequence; a highlight of *Live and Let Die*. I practised taking a boat fast, at 20, then 30, then 40, then 50, then 60 miles an hour round sharp U-bends. These are not ordinary outboard-engined power-boats; they are jets. The steering can only be controlled when the motor is turning. Three times we made the same sharp bend and three times the engines cut out and picked up again. As we came round for the fourth time I said to the instructor with me in the boat: 'I wonder if it will cut out again.' Well, I pushed my luck and it did, and this time it didn't pick up again.

We limped back to shore with a badly holed boat and likewise body. I was piled into a car, still in my swimming shorts, and driven back to New Orleans. My teeth I felt were the most important, so I saw a dentist first. A quick X-ray showed a fractured front tooth which by then was hurting like mad. Then I was carted off to a clinic where the doctor gave me the good news that my leg wasn't broken and Luisa gave me the bad news that my pants were dirty. After what I had just gone through I wasn't the least bit surprised. I was taken back then to my hotel to reflect on the day's battle scars.

Thursday's mail brought an offer from *Cosmopolitan* to be their centre page pin-up for the June issue to coincide with the opening of *Live and Let Die*. Fame at last! Me to be the bunny for liberated ladies! Needless to say I was *not* about to pose in the altogether!

When I first knew I was going to do Bond, Harry Saltzman, who co-produces the bond series with Cubby Broccoli, said it must be kept top secret but he wanted me to meet the director, Guy Hamilton, away from the office where we would not be seen. We met at Scott's in Mayfair, in true Bond-style, over a dozen oysters and martinis. I confessed to Guy that in reading the script I could only ever hear Sean's voice saying: 'My name is Bond.' In fact, as I vocalized to myself I found that I was giving it a Scottish accent. Guy said: 'Look, Sean was Sean and you are you and that is how it is going to be.'

Friday, the thirteenth. The first day of shooting began for me at about 6.30 in the morning after a very bad night with my painful leg and aching shoulder and rattling teeth. I staggered out of bed and decided I'd do my work-out, which I could get through apart from the knees-bend because my knees wouldn't bend any more.

Pushed underneath the door was a little envelope. It was a note from Guy on French Quarter Inn notepaper. It was headed, 'Dawn. D-Day' and read: 'Into battle and very encouraged by your very kind note. Here's good fortune to us all. As ever, Guy.' The note he referred to was one I slipped under his door the night before saying: 'Good luck for the following day and go break a leg,' which I had nearly done, and I added: 'If I don't do what I am told you have my full permission to kick me up the backside.' I'm glad to say he didn't that day, but there are many more to come.

We were shooting about thirty miles outside New Orleans in a backwater bayou. Bond is escaping from the lethal lieutenants of Mr Big, the black malevolent mastermind who plans to bludgeon the Western powers with the way-out weapons of hard drugs and voodoo. The story sweeps from New York's Harlem through New Orleans to Doctor Kananga's sinister island of San Monique. We began to shoot the boat chase sequence today and fortunately I was shot – by the camera that is – sitting down in the boat, so my limp did not show. I had one nasty moment when, on a sharp bend, my boat headed for the camera boat with Guy and about fifteen other people sitting in it. They were anchored there but they seemed to be tearing towards me rather like the corrugated iron shed had. I thought: 'Here we go again,' but I managed to come round on the wheel and pull away. I fully expected Guy to bawl at me when I got back, but he was very nice and said: 'Great, great.'

Luisa and a handful of us including Harry lunched in an air-conditioned roadside café. Outside it was about ninety degrees as I washed my Creole shrimps down with Michelob, a very nice light American beer. Harry, and Jackie his wife, were helping theirs down with a white wine, but Harry was screaming because it wasn't the Chablis he had ordered to be put on ice and the poor little serving lady was running round in circles.

Lunch over we got back to the boats. The water is dirty and slimy so that when we back up and rev the motors mud just churns up and the stench is awful. The water is all covered with nasty still green algae and you can see black snakes slithering through it. They put me at ease by telling me that the alligators were rather tired in this particular area so they wouldn't be likely to bite.

Jerry Comeaux, the boat organizer and stuntman, had to whip off his shirt three or four times and dive in to clear the duck weed out of the back of the jets. He was in and out amongst the slithering snakes and the filthy mud. But when the sun started to go down it was really a rather beautiful location.

Day One was done with, so I limped out of my boat back to my beautiful motor home, as they call it, sixteen thousand dollars' worth of home-on-wheels. I changed into my civvies and went back to the French Quarter Inn, to a large Jack Daniels with Branch water. Not water from the branch of the bayou I was in today, thank goodness.

Day Two. D-Day plus one, or B-Day for Bond plus one. It's my birthday. Happy birthday. Waking up this Saturday morning to the six o'clock alarm was a nasty shock. I limped round the room on my paralysed leg trying to do my morning work-out. I was in such a black mood I started giving Luisa hell. She wasn't at fault. I suppose I was resenting the fact that my leg was hurting and she hadn't mentioned the fact it was my birthday.

This morning I decided I needed my favourite laxative cereal, All-Bran. Room service seemed determined *not* to understand when I asked for All-Bran. 'All-what?' said a deep-Southern voice over the telephone. The head waiter settled it with, 'Give him a bowl of cornflakes.' Luisa handed me my case and as I took it by the handle it fell open scattering everything. She scooped the things back and I slammed out with, 'You didn't even remember it was my birthday.'

Harry Saltzman and I drove together to the location thirty miles outside New Orleans. It is deep in the swamp

13

country; beautiful, but a breeding ground for mosquitoes, alligators and snakes.

When we got to today's location there were two dozen-odd boats waiting for us and a pontoon; not the Twenty-one Blackjack variety but one which bobs up and down on the bayou. We moved off deep into the jungle like Sanders of the River. Today we were shooting a sequence where Jimmy Bond, that's me of course, is chased by three of the villain's boats. It was quite simple. It just meant sixty miles an hour cut-ins and swerves around the bayou finishing up with hair-raising jumps. Not the real big jumps. They are yet to come.

My limp matches that of Jimmy Cagney's as The Gimp, so it's as well my early scenes are all in the boat. If I had to walk I'm afraid shooting would stop, unless they found someone to do the walking for me.

Naturally Luisa didn't join us today. Harry let word slip as we were coming to the location that she was laying on something for my birthday. I'm not supposed to know but I have a feeling it is going to be a surprise party. I'm afraid I have a surprise for Luisa. I know Harry is finding a doctor this evening who is going to try and straighten my leg out. The hot water treatment I have been having has not been exactly successful. All it has done is make my leg red and bloated.

The only relief of a day spent sitting in a hundred degrees of mosquito-infested swamp was to get back to some nice baked American ham in the air-conditioned home-on-wheels which is my dressing room. We keep the ice box stacked high with fresh, pure mineral water since I discovered that Mel, our home-on-wheels driver, is a fellow kidney sufferer. Mine started thirteen years ago when I made a picture in the Utah desert. The picture was *The Gold of the Seven Saints* with Clint Walker. We were shooting out in the desert where the heat was 120 degrees and there was no shade. I got dehydrated. A year later the

14

problems started as a result of the dehydration and I began making kidney stones. In fact, two and a half years ago, just before I began *The Persuaders!*, I had major surgery and two stones were removed. Oddly enough, Maurice Woodruff the astrologer told me three months before I even made the picture in Utah and before I knew I was going to do it, that I would make a film in great discomfort, with a lot of heat, near water, and as a result of the heat I would suffer for many years.

Mine is not the only birthday on the set today. It is also the birthday of Derek Cracknell, the First Assistant, and Bill, one of the American grips. I knew it was Bill's birthday because I carefully placed a big cigar – out of which I had only had two puffs – down on the floor of the boat while I got into another one. When I looked for it again I caught sight of Bill, grinning and waving my great big stogie. I can take a hint. Happy birthday, Bill.

The place where we are shooting today is part of the great state of Louisiana, which is known as the sportsman's paradise. It is the mosquitoes who get all the sport, picking us up and spitting us out. Somebody told me they saw a mosquito carrying a sparrow. I know it's not true because I saw it. It was a pigeon.

Yesterday, the first day, I felt rather like a new boy with the crew because most of them had worked together before. It took them a day to discover that I wasn't completely chicken. They really are a great crew. The director, Guy, and Bob Kindred, the camera operator, tied themselves on the front of a boat today tearing at sixty miles an hour up and down the bayou photographing close-up reactions of me. That takes a lot of guts. It was then I knew why they wanted me to practise with the boats before commencement of principal photography; not so much for my safety, but more for theirs!

*   *   *

Monday morning and Day Three. Harry called me at eight to tell me we were going to a funeral. 'That's nice. Mine?' I queried. It turned out he meant a jazz funeral for a famous musician, Sylvester George Handy, who was being buried at 12 o'clock. I was on 'stand-by' which means I could be called out to the location where the rest of the unit were shooting at any moment if they needed me. The best laid plans of mice and men— They did and I had to tear out to the location in a great rush and never did get to the funeral. Undoubtedly I will get to my own.

So there I was again roaring up and down the bayou with the villains in hot pursuit, plus the mosquitoes. I'd rather face the villains. The organization of the boat chase is vast and varied. It will take over two weeks to shoot the eight minutes of final film which will appear on the screen. Luisa was with me and spent the whole day juggling a Nikormat with a 200 zoom lens and looking beautiful. She is helping me by illustrating this book and a few papers around the world. She's not just a pretty face.

A colossal crane moved in to lift ramps into place. I am about to jump the road at seventy-five miles an hour and we have been stopping traffic on this section of the road where we have a car parked with a great motor boat sticking right through it. It is used in one of the sequences where the villain's boat doesn't make the jump over the road to the other water and piles straight into the sheriff's car.

I am going to call Guy, our director, the General from now on. He is the complete commander in the field deploying his troops. There must be more than a hundred people on our unit and to get them all working together is no mean feat, especially in this heat. We did a shot this afternoon where a speed boat sails forty feet through the air and watching the General organize this stunt was really something. Clifton James, who plays the red-neck sheriff, and Tommy Lane, who plays Adam, one of the villains, have to stand between the two stretches of water while the boat

16

zooms over their heads. I told John, the Wardrobe, to go and tell the sheriff that he needed his hat for a minute to put some Kleenex in it, just in case the boat hits him.

Everybody takes it in great spirit. We drew a crowd of thousands here today. I hope they are not like some crowds at airports who don't go to see the planes land but to see them crash.

Double top marks to the stunt men on this picture. I have never seen anything like the two jumps Jerry Comeaux, the ace stunt boat driver, did today. He was doubling for one of the black actors and wearing a Robertson's marmalade wig and black face. On the second jump he took off on a forty feet leap, hit the water, skidded in the wake of another boat and flipped up on to the bank. Everybody, including myself, rushed forward. The First Assistant was screaming, 'Get back. I didn't say anybody could get into the shot.' The cameras were still turning. Happily, Jerry was all in one piece; his wig must have saved him.

He came back with me to my home-on-wheels where I had some Jack Daniels waiting for him and a nurse to examine the base of his spine which was hurting. As some-body helped him off with his wet suit the trousers he was wearing underneath came down exposing his rear end. He let out a scared shout. The tough guy was embarrassed about the nurse seeing his winkle. I told him what John Barrymore once said to Anthony Quinn: 'How can I be proud of that in which every chimpanzee is my equal and every jackass my superior?'

B-Day Four and we seem to be dogged by bad luck. It is either a gremlin or someone from SMERSH trying to sabotage Jimmy Bond's activities. Yesterday there was Jerry who limped out still smiling from under his upturned boat and today it was the turn of one of the other boat drivers, John Kerner. He was with me in the boat when I smashed my leg up and escaped with a cut chin. This time he was not so lucky. One of the wires holding the boat to the sheriff's car snapped and the flying wire caught him in the eye. It looks like they will have to operate. I wonder who will be next?

I am on 'stand-by' again today. It is a privilege I enjoy because it means I don't have to sit around the set all day long doing nothing. Joel Rosen, our Second Assistant Director, who signs himself 'Your favourite Assistant' when he arranges a stand-by call for me, phoned to say I was clear for the day. Luisa, Jackie, Harry and I took off to explore the French Quarter. It is a beautiful part of New Orleans with more art and curio shops, museums and restaurants than there are homes. The centre is Bourbon Street which is very hot in the day and very sleazy. There are strip joints with real girls; strip joints with boy-girls and strip joints with just boys, as well as a lot of good jazz joints.

We lunched in a Chinese restaurant called China Town which was something of a new experience. Like the joke about the man who went into a restaurant and ordered the entire meal in Chinese and the waiter was amazed because it was a French restaurant. In this Chinese restaurant the waitress was, for a start, Black. Harry, a fastidious eater and somewhat of a gourmet, was suspicious of a Chinese restaurant on Bourbon Street and looked quizzically at the menu. Suddenly a look of horror crossed his face. 'Is that the cook?' he queried, peering towards the kitchen from where a very black face beamed back. 'Oh, no, sir,' came the reply. 'That's one of our waiters. The owner is the cook and he *is* Chinese.'

I spent the afternoon in a very expensive fashion playing gin rummy with Harry. I have a feeling he only asks me to play to get my salary back.

* * *

Wednesday: B-Day five. At breakfast I watched television; a horrifying amount of twaddle is served up at the breakfast hour. A small group of actresses and fringe show business people make the constant round of chat shows telling the same stories day after day, particularly the mid European sisters who I will refrain from naming but they are darlinks, darlinks, darlinks. These ladies really enjoy talking about themselves. It is a mystery to me how the interviewer manages to look interested. I would rather spend the day in the swamp with the mosquitoes.

Today we shot more of the boat sequence. The drama of the boat chase is relieved by the humorous character of Sheriff Pepper who really gets the mickey taken out of him. Clifton James gives a beautiful performance as the Sheriff. One of the unit drivers was once a member of the local police force and he managed to get hold of a copy of the script to show the real local sheriff. It says a lot for the hospitality and cooperation of the New Orleans police force that he didn't have us thrown out of Louisiana. The Metropolitan police, or any other English police force, would not have taken such a send-up so kindly.

Unfortunately, it was a long lunch hour. Surprise, surprise, Harry had brought his cards and I paid for another day's shooting. He is now talking about the second Bond, *The Man with the Golden Gun* to begin shooting in August next year; financed presumably out of the money I will owe him when this one is over.

Sad to say our screenwriter, Tom Mankiewicz, has gone back to California. We'll miss his smiling face but he could be back. General Hamilton says we might run into some screen play crisis in Jamaica, our next location. Tom, who co-wrote *Diamonds Are Forever*, is the son of that great writer, producer, director, Joe Mankiewicz, who has just finished *Sleuth* in London with Laurence Olivier and Michael Caine.

Cloudy weather held up the afternoon's shooting so I was

interviewed by a reporter from the local *Dixie Rota*; a very pretty young lady called Jennifer with a 'Y'all and shut ma mouth' accent. Remind me to tell Tony Curtis that she had not heard of *The Persuaders!* She seemed doubtful that we had seen alligators nearby, although I told her we had seen one that very morning and it asked what time she was coming out.

B-Day Six started in the early morning dark humidity of Conti Street outside the French Quarter Inn where the *Plymouth Fury III* waited. We wound our way up through Jackson Square to the French Market, the Covent Garden of New Orleans, our headlights picking up pumpkins ready for morning buyers, some already decorated for Hallowe'en. We sped out under the concrete pylons holding up the interstate highway to Slidell as the morning mist over the swamps and bayous slowly yielded to the yellow sun. Streaks of grey cloud threatened rain; a seventy per cent possibility today according to the radio.

Harry has bought me some espresso coffee. My Italian wife has accustomed me to coffee Italian-style; three cups and you don't sleep for a week. Fred Goldberg, who I have to say is a very nice man because he is Vice President in charge of Advertising and Publicity for United Artists, who back and release the Bond films world wide arrived today from New York bringing me two boxes of Jamaican cigars. He *is* a very nice man. Speaking of cigars, I still have my secret supply of Havanas I smuggled through American customs.

John Kerner, one of the boat organizers, who got a piece of wire in his eye, rejoined the unit today after surgery. The keenness of him and everybody else to get to work is admirable.

Jerry Comeaux and I cruised upstream to go over the course for the day's chase and by half past nine we had been greeted by two alligators, three cottonmouth moccasins and a hell of a lot of jumping trout. The only reptile of these parts which I haven't met so far is the Copper Head. They are as poisonous as a rattle snake so I have no wish to expedite an introduction.

I had a surprise visitor today on the set. Bob Dix, son of that famous actor, Richard Dix. We were under contract at MGM one hundred and fifty years ago. Since those days he has produced nine films, married three times and has a couple of kids. My mother would be absolutely gaga if she could see Bob Dix because he looks exactly like his father who was her favourite screen heart-throb. When I was a child she used to take me to see all his pictures. My father was mad for Jean Harlow and I was just mad for ice-cream and Mickey Mouse.

Disaster was averted when the pontoon carrying, if you'll pardon the pun, twenty-one people was swept out of control in a wide, strong current. The water was slapping over the side and everybody was nervously clutching scripts, cameras and cans of film. Jerry and I felt suitably heroic when we saved the day by pushing the bows of our power-boat up against the pontoon and shunted it out of trouble.

Elaine, the script girl, dubbed 'The Duchess', was already jittery but really got the wind-up when I said we hadn't seen an alligator for at least five minutes.

Harry cornered me at lunch time for our floating gin rummy game and this time I broke even, which is like winning when you are playing with Harry. He left early in a glum mood because he has to pay today's production costs out of his own pocket. Or perhaps it was because I stirred it up by telling him that whatever our stunt driver, Jerry Comeaux, was being paid for his fifty foot leaps, it was not enough and that I had told Jerry the same and advised him to get an agent.

The *Live and Let Die* circus is really beginning to catch on in these parts. Our caravan of spectators gets larger and larger. I spend more time signing autographs than I do chasing villains. The threatened rain didn't come but it is decidedly cooler. It makes a pleasant change from the sauna bath conditions in which we have been working.

The lawns of the Baldwin estate sweep down to the bayou's edge where at low tide the wreck of a Union Army barge is revealed. Soft Spanish moss decorates the giant oak trees and makes a picturesque setting for B-Day Seven.

The peace was shattered by the roar of Evinrude engines as Bond's boat, with me at the wheel, leaps out of the water up on to the lawn, closely followed by one of the villains whose boat outstrips mine and lands in the swimming pool. A power boat with a 135 hp Evinrude sitting in a kidney-shaped swimming pool on somebody's lawn is a ludicrous sight. It looks like one of those advertisements for the man who has everything.

To get a back view of me at the wheel, General Hamilton and Bob, the camera operator, planted themselves in the boat's back seat. This upset the delicate balance and when Guy said, 'Hit it' I gunned the engine, the nose came up and stayed up under their weight and we skidded along for 300 yards at an angle of 90 degrees with the water and our backsides submerged. Next time we weighted the bows down with sand bags.

Cubby Broccoli joined us today from London bringing with him Donald Zec of the *Daily Mirror*. For Donald it was a totally unexpected trip. The day before Cubby had suggested they have dinner and Donald agreed. Cubby said: 'I have booked a table at Antoine's in New Orleans.' A slightly bewildered Donald flew 4,000 miles from London for a meal which, he assures me, was probably worth it.

Tomorrow we shoot a wedding scene in which Bond, pursued by villains, roars in a speed-boat across a 200 yard-long lawn where a bridal pair are taking their vows. Alas, the local radio picked up the news and wrongly announced that we needed extra wedding guests. It will be chaos.

The spot where we shoot tomorrow is where I came in conflict with the corrugated iron shed when we were rehearsing. Thinking of that accident reminds me of another. It was in my very first starring role in Hollywood with Lana Turner. The picture was *Diane*, the story of Diane de Poitiers, played by Lana. I was Henry II of France. Dressed in magnificent golden armour I led a charge of sixty horsemen. My gauntlets, like my breastplate, were metal and would not bend easily. As I spurred the horse forward I lost the reins and just managed to kick my feet free from the stirrups as the beast charged straight for some stone steps. I became conscious under a circle of worried faces and muttering voices. The first clear words which came to my ears were Lana's. They were: 'Is it all right?'

B-Day Eight and in front of an outdoor altar on the rolling lawns of the Treadway estate the movie marriage that, we hope, will never be consummated is being solemnized. The bayou flows peacefully by and a nuptial nicety hangs in the air like the soft Spanish moss from the circling trees. But the beautiful bride, the groom, the bridesmaids, the vicar and eighty wedding guests seem too tense for a languid, sunny Southern wedding. Not surprising.

The tranquillity was torn by the horrendous roar of power which drowned the marriage vows; four cameras turned and rows of stills cameras prepared to click as the jet boats, stunt driver Murray Cleveland in the lead, hit the bank at sixty-five miles per hour. Murray skidded wildly across the lawn out of control and crunched straight into a giant oak tree with the loudest thud I have ever heard. The cameras stopped as Murray was thrown forwards then backwards and a mob of people ran to pull him clear. Ten minutes later Jerry Comeaux's boat lost power and crashed into another tree; and as if two accidents were not enough for the day, the engine on a third boat cut and it also careered into a tree.

After a forty-five minute delay, stunt coordinator, Eddie Smith, aimed his boat with unerring accuracy at over sixty miles an hour, leaping from the water on to the lawn and slid straight for the three-tiered wedding cake. The bows burst the cake into a cloud of confectionery while the boat ripped on into the wedding reception marquee, shattering tables, chairs, piled presents and champagne glasses; all ending in an ear-splitting special effects bang.

The Treadway estate which once formed part of an Indian reservation, looked like Custer's cavalry had been on the rampage. Behind the collapsed marquee casualties were spread out like a field hospital. The three wrecked boats make it an expensive day for the insurance companies: £30,000 down the drain, or should I say, the bayou. Still, the doctors of America are having a field day.

I took Donald Zec out in one of the boats for a quiet, slow cruise before lunch. Having seen the accidents I don't think he was very happy about it but it gave him an appetite because we had only been out five minutes when he dropped some very deliberate hints about having lunch. The production's upper echelon was sitting in a semi-circle on the lawn. Harry got up and walked away prompting Donald to ask where he had gone. 'The way things are going today,' I said, 'I think he's gone to *shul*.'

Tension was running high between the Press and stills photographers who were squabbling among themselves about which of them should have what pictures. I spend much of my day listening to 'Could you move over here, please'; 'Look up at this light'; and 'Watch this lens, please'. It reminds me of when Luisa and I got married at Caxton Hall. Every day brings new journalists and there are so many here now they outnumber the mosquitoes. The pressure of being Bond grows daily. Not in playing the part

24

but in being the actor playing the part. How much time am I going to be able to spend actually acting?

I could not sleep last night and finally fell into a fitful doze at 2 AM, only to be awakened at 5 AM by Leslie Bricusse calling from London where it was only 11 AM. He has saved a piece of the investment in his new show *The Good Old Bad Old Days* for me. Leslie has written a number of lyrics for the Bond films title songs and Cubby is anxious to talk to him about a lyric for *Live and Let Die*. When I got back from location tonight I turned on the television and there was Leslie's wife, Yvonne Romaine. So the Bricusse family started and ended my day. The sun goes up, the sun goes down.

Sunday morning and Day Nine; and up comes television's verbal mush with my breakfast marmalade. I searched the channels for an early newscast but all I could get were words like: 'I felt like crying, my heart was sad, just everything, I mean, it's tough to put into words but I looked into his eyes and he looked like he wanted to cry and I felt the same. I just wanted to touch him and just let him know that I was with him at that particular moment. It takes a real man to do that.' This was an interview between a sports commentator and a sportsman. It is too much to take at any time and impossible at 6 AM.

In spite of yesterday's disasters two boats and two of our willing Kamekaze characters, the stunt drivers, were ready to shoot the rest of the wedding party sequence on the Treadways' lawns. At the crack of dawn the unit convoyed to the Irish Bayou but there was to be no shooting. It was impossible to see where the bayou began and the Treadways' lawns ended; their rolling green grass had disappeared under three feet of water. Strong winds had whipped the 610 square miles of Lake Pontchartrain which lies to the north of New Orleans and pushed water back into the bayous swamping the lawns. The flood is an expensive business for Cubby and Harry; with costs running at something like 70,000 dollars a day filming is not casually cancelled.

Dollars apart, I was delighted to have a rest day but I expect the eighty-four friends of the Treadways who had decked themselves out in their finery ready for the washed out wedding scene were disappointed. Luisa and Keri, Guy's wife Kerima, dragged me off for a busman's holiday in the afternoon to the local cinema.

Work-wise the day was not completely wasted. I was able to get into some of my Bond clothes, the Roger Moore/ Cyril Castle designed suits I wear, and wander off through the streets of the French Quarter with Akhtar Hussein, the photographer, and George Whitear, our unit photographer, for a New Orleans photo session. You have no idea what an idiot you feel standing wearing a black, silk safari suit in the middle of the day in Bourbon Street with tourists gawking at you while you pose for the photographers.

'Champagne' Charlie Slater, who owns the French Quarter Inn, threw a party for his twenty-second wedding anniversary last night and invited all the unit staying here. General Guy dropped out because he has to be up so early but, being the one actor of the group, I was expected to be there. We ventured out into the grand, very expensive suburb of Gretna where the millionaires of New Orleans have their homes.

Charlie lives on splendid scale and style and being the owner of a very expensive hotel the catering was superb. Tables groaned under lobster soufflés, shrimps with Louisiana mustard sauce, turkeys, legs and shoulders of lamb, racks of beef and giant American hams. The fun part of the evening came when a young lady got me into a corner and in an urgent whisper asked me: 'Are the broads loose in Scotland?' Naturally I had to make her repeat it because I could not quite believe my ears but I had heard right the first time. Her problem was her husband was off to Scotland

and she was anxious he should come back with the knowledge not of what Scotsmen wore under their kilts, but rather their lassies.

I have become a sadist; a step in the right direction for assuming the complete character of Jimmy Bond. How and why did this sadistic streak emerge?

Today's shooting: B-Day Ten, needed a lot of preparation and rehearsal. Clifton James as Sheriff Pepper leading five cars in a one hundred miles an hour chase down Louisiana's Highway Eleven, gets the shock of his life as two jet boats zoom from one stretch of water to another across the road straight in front of his speeding patrol car.

I was not in the shot so while equipment was shifted around, the mobs of sightseers shunted to one side, I was pushed into a power boat with my phalanx of photographers from the world's press in hot pursuit and sent off to some corner of the bayou that is forever swampy and mosquito-infested. Daily, more of the mechanics behind the mystique that is Bond become clear. The actual shooting, the rapport between my countenance and the camera, forms only a fraction of a field of operations which is a constant source of surprise. Our already crowded unit increases day by day as we are joined by photographers, television crews and documentary film crews from all corners of the world. This morning we have newcomers from the National Dairy Council shooting a commercial for release in British cinemas showing that film-makers the world over drink milk between takes.

We also have a television unit from NBC Television. There was not enough room in the camera boat for them all at the same time so they had to come out in relays, which meant I had to go through all the action, leaping waves and haring round bends repeatedly until they had all captured it for posterity.

It was about half an hour before lunch when the moment of sadistic inspiration came. I suggested they should stay in a fixed position while Tommy Lane, who plays one of the black baddies, and myself made motor boat passes before their battery of lenses. Little did they suspect the fiendish plan afoot. Two hundred yards from their bobbing boat Tommy and I swept our power jets in a tight forty miles per hour arc then, with me in the lead, we bore down at a screeching sixty miles an hour. Barely a boat's length from them I threw the wheel over hard and piled on all the power I had. A mountain of musky bayou spume and slime shot up and cascaded over the cameramen. What a marvellous game! I politely inquired if they had got the shot before belting back to base to collect the next photographers for a soaking. Sadistic, maybe, but I tell myself it is essential I get into character.

Soft and dirge-like, the rhythm of drums accompanying muted trombone and trumpet, the Olympia Brass Band filed funeral fashion down Bourbon Street this morning under a grey and sombre sky. Two official mourners, shuffling and side-stepping to the mournful music, led the cortège, sashes emblazoned across their chests. A traditional New Orleans jazz funeral with only one thing missing – the body.

In *Live and Let Die* it is provided by an unwary CIA agent who asks whose funeral it is. 'Yours' comes the reply as an assassin whips out a knife. Bob Dix, my old friend who turned up on the set last week, is playing Hamilton, the CIA agent, because when Guy saw him his immediate reaction was that he was exactly right for the part. Poor Bob. Little did he know what he was in for. Veteran jazzman, 'Kid' Thomas Valentine from Preservation Hall, shrine of jazz purists, is playing the assassin. His splendid row of gold teeth contrasting beautifully with his dark skin and large mouth, which will look absolutely marvellous on the large screen, make him perfect for the part. But he was not too sure where to stick the knife. Bob has padding underneath his jacket but the assassin couldn't hit the right spot. The weathermen threatened a seventy per cent chance of rain and before thirty per cent of the day had gone a torrential downpour put paid to Day Eleven's filming. Bob may seriously consider whether he wants to go on with the role when we come back to shoot the rest of the sequence.

I went off to get rid of one of my countless interviews for the day during lunch, looking for a restaurant in the French Quarter with Luisa trotting along behind getting sopping wet, plus a couple of journalists and a photographer.

There is nothing more depressing for a director keyed up for an important scene with a vast number of people involved and all sorts of technical implications to worry about, than to have the weather turn against him. When I am wearing my director's hat I am always unlucky with the weather. The first time I ever directed a 'Saint' episode was in the pouring rain. I remember it particularly clearly because Luisa was six months pregnant at the time. I was shooting on the back lot of EMI-MGM at Boreham Wood, near London, with Oliver Reed and Imogen Hassall. The set was a Greek village post office and it was what we call an interior/exterior set. That is to say the set was built in the open air with no roof on it so I could shoot inside the post office with natural light thus cutting the cost of using highly-priced lighting equipment. As I stood there inside the post office, trying to direct the scene with rain pelting in through the open roof, the producer, Bob Baker, called me aside to a dry spot and broke the news that Luisa had been taken to the London Clinic with labour pains. I nearly passed out on the spot and rain on location still reminds me of that moment. Thank God, the doctors were able to prevent her miscarrying and three months later we were blessed with Deborah, my nine-year-old daughter, who at this moment along with my six-year-old Geoffrey, I miss desperately. I spoke to Deborah on the telephone today and she is counting the days when she and Geoffrey will be here with us. They arrive in three days time. I haven't spoken to them since I left home because I get too depressed thinking of them so far away.

Our ranks are beginning to swell as various crew members' wives turn up. I am a great believer in having the family around because it makes for earlier nights. On locations where all the crew are wifeless they congregate in the local bar, get smashed out of their minds, stay up far too late and work the next day suffers because they feel bloody awful. Tony Curtis and I had our wives with us when we made *The Persuaders!* in the South of France, as did several of the crew members who looked on a little enviously as their bachelor mates went off for the evening but laughed hysterically when the fun seekers had to wait five days for a medical clearance.

Today's rain dampened the fiery outbursts which were erupting on the set. Everybody was shouting at everybody. Harry shouted at Derek, Guy shouted at Harry, Derek shouted at Dan, the unit publicist, journalists shouted at each other; nobody shouted at me, not even Luisa. I had my turn yesterday when Harry exploded. I had climbed into one of the power-boats to take Luisa, and David Hedison who has just joined us to play Felix Leiter, for a spin. Harry told me to take one of the boat experts with me. What he thinks I am I don't know; I have done death-defying stunts in the boat already but for a pleasure spin he feels someone should come with me! He apologized over lunch for blowing his cool and said he'd had a bad morning with various union bosses who seem to control the making of motion pictures nowadays.

Guy's clash with Harry came because the vast circus of publicity is getting under the General's skin. Christopher Doll, who is making a television documentary on the film tried time and time again to get the five black stunt men together in a boat for an interview and each time he was ready to shoot they were called back on set. Guy was screaming loud because he was kept waiting at one end of the bayou while they were at the other. The Publicity Department problems start at the bottom. A locally hired secretary cracked under the pressure and was last seen disappearing through the door swearing she would not feed 'that god damned baby alligator' they keep as an office mascot.

It's nice to have David Hedison as Bond's CIA buddy, Felix Leiter. We met in Hollywood years ago when he was making *The Fly* with Vincent Price. It was a science-fiction story about a fly with a man's head and David, in the title role, had a last line of 'Help me. Help me' delivered in a squeaky, high-pitched voice. I always greet him with my own falsetto version of his line. By a curious coincidence *The Fly* was shown on television the day David arrived in New Orleans.

To my horror on the set the other day I heard Harry bawling 'Nigger'. He was not trying to start a race riot but simply calling to our English props man 'Nigger' Weymouth, a nickname he has answered to since the days of silent cinema. I pointed out that it might be better to find him another name here in the racial hotbed of Louisiana so we have settled on 'Chalky'. As Bond, I make love to Rosie Carver, played by beautiful black actress, Gloria Hendry, and Luisa has learned from certain Louisiana ladies that if there is a scene like that they won't go to see the picture. I personally don't give a damn and it makes me all the more determined to play the scene.

Harry joined David and me for dinner at Kolb's, a German restaurant where incongruous black waiters serve sauerkraut, wiener schnitzel and all the other schnitzels, as well as lager in the traditional stein. These are so popular with customers that far too many get taken home and a security man has been installed to stop the thefts.

Noticing a customer walking out with a suspicious bulge under his coat he stopped him and asked to see what he was carrying. Pulling back his jacket the man revealed a wicked looking .45 calibre revolver and holster. He turned out to be a Jefferson Parish deputy sheriff.

Harry has a nasty habit of walking into a restaurant and demanding whether the service is quick and, of course, they always say it is. When the soup arrives he says it is cold and sends it back, so it is advisable to hold on to your soup plate as soon as it arrives or he sends yours back too. Cubby Broccoli says that if Harry had been at the Last Supper he would have sent that back.

The cancelled shooting today deprived me of a moment of glory – I was due to say my first two words as James Bond. Although we have been shooting for two weeks it has all been hectic action and my carefully rehearsed delivery of the two words 'Where's Strutter?' has been delayed. Contrary to what the wags are saying this will not be the first silent Bond.

Friday, 27 October. No shooting today and the bliss of a lie-in. After yesterday's disastrous torrential rains Harry, prompted by the bad weather forecast as well as the fact that it was his birthday, rescheduled and made today a rest day. He has gone to relatives in Florida with Jackie and his three children, Steven, Hilary and Christopher. It was the wrong decision because we were greeted by sunny skies when we woke this morning.

We lunched with film producer, Elliott Kastner and Tessa Kennedy who had arrived from Los Angeles with the two children the night before. Tessa is an interior decorator and is currently conferring with Luisa on the dining-room of our Denham home which she is doing for us. I left the two of them eagerly picking their way through a pile of materials marked 'Sale' in a French Quarter fabric shop and went off to book a table at The Court of Two Sisters, a picturesque restaurant in an open, tree-ringed courtyard.

If there is one thing I cannot stand it is the open-handed head waiter and this place had one. His beady eyes raked me from top to toe taking in my lack of tie and casual denim outfit. He could not reserve a table but if we came in at one PM he would 'look after me', he said as his face lit lugubriously and his hand slid into a suitable position to be greased with a five dollar bill. We lunched instead at Brennans, where the management were straightforward charm itself and plied us with free wine and aperitifs, but I must have had a bad ice cube because I got stinking drunk and returned to bed for the afternoon.

Day Twelve and back to work. Paul Rabiger, our make-up man, was telling me about other Bond films he has done while he was working on me this morning. He has been on every one except the first – *Dr No* – and consequently has made up all the leading ladies; and when you meet a girl every morning at around 7 AM without her make-up it's like being married to her.

Paul's favourite Bond girls were Jill St John and Honor Blackman. Whenever I hear Honor's name I remember her brother, Steve Black, who was in my unit in the army. He looked like her but unfortunately he died a couple of years after he came out of the army. Very tragic.

Speaking of leading ladies, Paul agrees with Guy, Tom Mankiewicz and myself that it would have been more interesting if Solitaire, our present leading lady, had been black as she was in Tom's original screen play, but United Artists would not stand for it.

We talked about all the bad men of the Bond films Paul has helped create. His most difficult task was a mask for Charles Gray in *Diamonds are Forever* because the face actually had to look *like* Charles. Donald Pleasence's menacing make-up in *You Only Live Twice* included one eye virtually closed except for one small glimmer of blue.

'You know those round, blue eyes that he makes,' said Paul, 'he only had one and the other one used to do the best it could through that little aperture.'

Talking of long Bond picture association with Paul brought us to Lois Maxwell, our Miss Moneypenny, who has been in all of them, and Bernard Lee, Bond's boss, M. But there is doubt whether Bernard, because of personal reasons, will appear in this one. I hope he does. Kenneth More asked me to tell Harry and Cubby that he would play M and they could send the fee to Bernard which is a very gentlemanly gesture. Our co-producers said they will take care of him anyway. Paul said that a hairdresser on the last Bond picture was taken ill after she had been hired, but before the picture had started shooting. She only worked the last week but they paid her throughout. Crew bonuses are not unknown and Paul told me he got £250 on one picture.

Today was another day of driving around in boats without a line of dialogue. My recurring nightmare is that when I do have a line to say I am going to forget the damned thing. We covered a key shot of the boat chase sequence today in a boatyard at Slidell where Adam the heavy, played by Tommy Lane, meets a spectacular end. A tank landing craft, its ramp down leaving a gaping hole in its hull, waits like a giant hungry whale to gulp Adam into its iron intestines.

This shipyard with its vast expanse of water and acres of huge rusting wrecks would be impossible to reproduce in a studio. Our speed-boats slide and roar round the narrow channels and it takes some doing. Because of engine noise and distance, Tommy Lane, the other black villains and myself, are in touch with the General and camera crews by walkie-talkie. But I confess I have not understood one word of radio direction yet; something the General does not know. Muffled voices scream 'Go, go, go!' but I never know if they are talking to me, the other drivers or the camera boat. I just put my faith in my boat and aim for one of the eight-foot gaps hoping for the best. Today as we whipped between the boats the bobbing raft holding the camera crew took the full force of my wash and every man among them was soaked from head to foot, not to mention water-logged cameras. I got drenched which is something I tried to dodge because I ache in every bone and I feel symptoms of the 'flu or some other lousy lurgy.

The children arrive tomorrow and I wonder if Geoffrey will realize that I *am* Bond when he sees me in action. Just before we left England he asked:

'Can you beat anybody, including a robber?'

'Oh, yes,' I replied confidently.

'Supposing James Bond came in,' he persisted.

'Daddy is going to play James Bond,' I explained.

'I know that,' he sighed impatiently. 'I mean the *real* James Bond, Sean Connery.'

Sunday, the Thirteenth B-day and a beautiful morning in more ways than one. Last night I went to bed at seven P M on a bowl of onion soup to sweat my way through three pairs of pyjamas and a couple of towelling dressing-gowns to shake what the crew are calling bayou 'flu and this morning the 'flu has flown. Another day at the boat-yard and a beautiful morning work-wise because the first shot was in the can by 7.45 and by 'can' I mean film can and not the American colloquialism for lavatory pan. Beautiful weather, the sky seemed to have been brushed blue and white by Canaletto.

Mid-morning I posed for a coterie of stills cameramen with the Bond gun collection which consists of twenty-five assorted sidearms before being hauled away by Chris Doll. Chris is doing our documentary, which I have dubbed the 006 and seven-eighths saga, and had me talking to myself as I walked down a railway track which runs into the shipyard where we are shooting. The shot panned down the rail track as I mouthed a monologue feeling a total idiot.

The next encounter was with the dapper Senor Manolo Urquiza, a television personality from Puerto Rico. His card informed that his company was called, to my amazement and amusement, Ponce Television. We bobbed in a moored boat while he shot his interview, translating my replies into rapid Spanish.

The sequel to our early shot which showed me and Tommy Lane neck and neck in speed boats at thirty knots while I throw petrol at him was to be a gi-normous bang. I manoeuvre Tommy in line with the ramp of the tank landing craft and he shoots up it to a deafening death. Controlling the boat at high speeds through choppy waters with one hand, with Guy and a cameraman perched perilously on the bows, and throwing petrol with the other is not something I want to do every day. The big attraction for the Press today was the blast. Nobody would tell me how much explosive there was in the belly of the 325 feet tank landing craft. I was not on camera during the explosion shot so Dan Slater, the British publicist, came up with the bright idea of seating me casually before the photographers, glass of white port held Bond-style in my hand, gazing nonchalantly away from the explosion about 300 yards away. I agreed but an hour later saw that the film camera crew had built a hide to protect themselves from the blast and flying debris.

'Why are you hiding behind there, fellows?' I asked foolishly.

'Well, Rarge,' said one of the American crew, 'they say there's gonna be a little blast.'

I hesitated even more when I heard Dan telling a journalist that I am insured for five million dollars. An Assistant Director suggested we move from the barge where the stills were planned to the opposite bank which seemed safer but was thirty yards nearer to the blast. But it would not be much good for the Bond image to chicken out, so there I sat, through the countdown, clutching a glass of chilled white port with the photographers on my right and all hell to be let loose on my left.

The bang came and I don't know if it blew me or I jumped four feet in the air, somehow without spilling one drop of wine. As a cool-in-a-crisis-Bond shot it could have been disaster, but most of the photographers leapt a bit higher than I did. A huge tongue of flame licked from the landing craft, smoke belched and the cameras clicked. A Swedish photographer thought it would be jolly if we strolled closer to the blaze as the bang was, in theory, over. We found the fire-boat in fast retreat and somebody hollered through a loud hailer: 'Get back! Get back!' There's another two hundred pounds of explosives on deck.' The fireworks had not finished, but it didn't seem to stop the photographers pressing for just one more.

The clocks went back an hour yesterday and to catch all the sunlight we have to start shooting an hour earlier and finish, or wrap as we say in the film business, an hour earlier. Today, B-Day Fourteen, we left the swamps and bayous and exploding ships for the civilized silence and sophistication of the Southern Yacht Club's marina on the shores of Lake Pontchartrain.

Saying goodbye to the bayous will be sad because of the lovely people we have met. The Schneiders who have been hospitality itself to the crew, Luisa and myself; the Treadways, who repeatedly had their lawn churned up when we skidded speed-boats and smashed wedding cakes. I wonder if the amiable Mr Treadway really knew what he was letting himself in for the day he met Guy, who first landed on his lawn during a location helicopter recce. The General had spotted the Treadway grounds from the air and they then looked, and later proved, ideal.

Today a forest of aluminium masts marks our new venue,

the marina, as the base for Southern Louisiana's yachting society and the roar and wash from our racing boats soon provoked impassioned fist-waving from yachtsmen and intervention by the gun-toting crew of a police launch. After speeding around for weeks at sixty and seventy miles an hour we were clipped to a five miles an hour crawl.

The captain of a coastguard cutter, the *Point Spencer*, was very obliging and agreed to manoeuvre his patrol boat into the background of our shot. At the end of the day the skipper, Robert Mitchell, invited me on board to meet his eight-man crew and mascot, a white poodle called Pierre resplendent in an emerald green collar with emerald nail varnish to match. I boarded the baby battleship with my inevitable entourage of photographers and in a flash they had whipped the cover away from a beefy 81 mm shell gun and 50 calibre machine gun and had me swinging them round in suitable 007-style picture poses.

Today is the fourteenth day I have played Bond before the cameras and momentous because I said my first lines. Last evening I went through the scene carefully committing it to memory and was word perfect when I arrived on set. I suggested to David Hedison (Felix Leiter, my CIA buddy in the film), sitting having his suntan evened off around the eyes with a make-up sponge, that we run through the scene, to discover that the lines he was saying were entirely different from those I had learned. 'What script are you using – *Diamonds Are Forever*? I asked him. Then I noticed the colour of his script pages. His were blue and mine were white; a very significant difference because the colours denote script changes. I had been given the changes but forgotten to insert them and the page and a half of dialogue I had mastered was reduced to: 'Hello, Felix. What are you doing here?' – my very first words as Bond, although not the first words Bond will say in the finished film. What were to be my first words: 'Where's Strutter?,' were eclipsed because the jazz funeral scene in which I said them was postponed because of rain.

Still, it is just one of those little things that happen with script changes. Sometimes scripts are changed so much, starting with blue for the first change, pink for the second change, yellow for the third change, that they run out of the rainbow and have to start all over again.

I am suffering from lack of sleep because my children arrived last night. They reached the hotel at ten past seven, by quarter past seven they were in bed, by twenty past seven they were asleep and at three o'clock they were awake asking for biscuits. London time is six hours ahead of New Orleans, so when they arrived at 7 PM it was 1 AM to them, having slept eight hours they woke at 3 AM feeling hungry. Three weeks is a long time in a child's life and they seem to have grown an inch for every week we have been away. My son has got so tall I called him 'Sir'.

I was not the only one under the weather today. One of the British crew members, who must remain anonymous for marital security reasons, looked worse for wear with an ugly welt across his face, after a night out in a topless-bottomless bar in Bourbon Street with some of his colleagues; my American driver, Al, acting as host. The bar's attraction is a lady on a swing whose high-button booted legs hurtle out at regular intervals through a tawdry curtain over the heads of passers-by in the street outside, while a loud-voiced tout shouts: 'Come in! Come in! See the girls naked! See the girls nude!' A rather buxom lady, who'd never heard of a Maidenform bra, was dancing on the bar among the mint juleps when my American driver leaned forward and tweaked her rear end. She turned in an absolute rage and smacked the first face she saw which belonged to our wide-eyed and innocent English crewman.

*   *   *

Tuesday, 31 October and another bayou for our fifteenth B-day of shooting. Eddie Smith, the ramrod, or leader of our black stunt men – a great looking bunch whose sparkling white tee shirts advertise 'Hollywood Black Stunt men' across their chests – had to zoom round a bend at seventy mph and skim under a very low bridge. Two days earlier at rehearsals his boat had cleared the underside of the bridge by an inch. The General and I were quietly chatting on the bank as Eddie roared round the bend straight for the bridge, ducking just in time as an ear-splitting crack filled the air. Heavy rain had raised the water level and, luckily for Eddie, it was only the windshield which smashed. The General's calm comment was: 'That was a bit bloody silly.'

Another of my black boating brothers, Tommy Lane, frequently gets an uncomfortable and scary ride bouncing about in my wash as he chases my boat, keeping the script-specified three boat lengths behind. Today was Tommy's turn to scare the hell out of someone else. I had completed a run when the walkie-talkie crackled and the General ordered Tommy into action. He had to take a bend at about fifty mph in his big black and chrome speed-boat. I heard a distant deep growl of Tommy's engine and looking over my shoulder saw the calm water split open as he hurtled into view. He missed the turn, catapulted up a grass bank and careered across a lawn toward the plate glass picture-window of a bayou-side bungalow. The casual gaze of the couple sedately sipping their elevenses turned into pop-eyed panic.

Scare stories abound today. Ted Moore, our normally imperturbable Director of Photography who holds the DFC and Croix de Guerre, barely twitched when someone yelled: 'Look out! A snake!' A dried-out snake skin was lying a few feet away. Minutes later frantic fingers pointed behind Ted and the holler: 'A snake! A snake!' went up again. Ted, without turning, smiled sagely, and said: 'Don't give me that.' Then the snake, about four feet long, slithered alongside him. He did a very uncharacteristic kangaroo leap. The funniest note of the day was struck by 'Chalky' Weymouth, our cockney top props man, who walked away shaking his head and muttering, 'That's the biggest jellied eel *I* ever saw.'

It is Hallowe'en and my children are going Trick or Treating tonight, a custom not shared by England. The children dress up in witches' costumes and funny make-up and go from door to door demanding, 'Trick or Treat?' and if they don't get a treat, a handful of sweets or something, they play a trick. Smearing your windows with soap is a favourite. Television is warning daily that children should not eat the sweets they are given until they have been examined by their parents, because some very strange people put things like razor blades in apples, poison in caramels and even LSD in sweets.

Home from location, a hot bath and a really nice cup of English tea, freshly brewed by Luisa. The absence of good tea on foreign locations can drive you mad, but a supply of Typhoo Tea has arrived. We use bottled water because tap water here is too chlorinated and we have our own little transportable stove in the hotel suite. So, but for the fact that we don't have the tennis court, the goldfish pond, the swimming pool, the woods, the pony and dog, we might just as well be at home.

The big brass from United Artists, no less than the President, David Picker, will be here in a couple of days. Harry says I have to dine with him, so maybe he is coming to fire me.

Wednesday 1 November. B-Day Sixteen. While much of Northern America freezes in snow storms and blizzards and London shivers awake to dark and drizzle, we sweat through long Louisiana days of eighty degree sunshine. We have said goodbye to the boats and the bayous and our flotilla of craft looks like it brushed with Nelson at his best. Out of thirty new speed-boats which sailed in from the showrooms, nineteen were write-offs and eleven badly battered. A well-kept secret concerning Murray Cleveland, one of the speed-boat stunt drivers, leaked last night as we left and prompted some leg-pulling. Murray, who has been working a seven day week, starting every day at 4.30 AM to bring the boats to the bayou and finishing at dusk, took time out on Sunday to speed through a quick marriage ceremony; his own.

Today we moved to Lake Front Airport, New Orleans, to commit the same kind of carnage on planes as we did on the boats. We have ten planes due for destruction although none of them will take to the air. Bond is caught, breaks free and is being hounded by car-loads of heavies at high speed round the hangars and runways. He escapes by commandeering a Cessna training plane complete with pupil passenger, a certain Mrs Bell, of middle years who believes Bond is her new instructor. Bond roars round the airport with the stupefied Mrs Bell beside him. Cars smash into planes, and a ramp has been built to send one careering over the tail of a parked DC3 passenger plane and we don't know where it will land.

The airport scene attracted more spectators today than any action to date. Our spectacular is being reported on Louisiana television, radio and the local Press, so tomorrow crowds could be worse and security will be tightened. The restrictions will be as much for spectators' safety as our convenience. The unit needs maximum clear room for man-oeuvre as one car cutting into a crowd out of control could have horrific results.

Our leading lady, Jane Seymour, who plays the virginal Solitaire, arrives tonight and her presence should take the journalistic heat off me as she will be a fresh and beautiful face for them to aim their lenses at and sharpen their pencils over. She is flying the same route as my children took, accompanied by my secretary Geraldine Gardner. They had their luggage turned over by Customs from top to bottom, from toys to typewriter, at Washington Airport. A six-year-old boy, a nine-year-old girl and a neatly groomed twenty-eight-year-old secretary are unlikely heroin, diamond, pot or potted plant smugglers. Disappointingly for Customs, no poppy seeds were found in Geoffrey's pop gun. I hope Jane doesn't get turned over by Customs. Come to mention it, if anybody is going to do any turning over with Jane, I would like it to be me, on screen of course, with due deference to Luisa.

I lunched with Syd Cain, our Production Designer, who is just back from Jamaica, our next location. Location catering in this country is something to be marvelled at. The menus include exotic dishes like barbecued spare ribs and stuffed cabbage leaves as well as superb beef stew and pork chops. Tables are set up under the trees in glorious surroundings and lunch is an elegant picnic; unlike English locations where you huddle in a doorway out of the blinding rain clutching a hot bacon sandwich.

Syd was telling me about the crocodile farm he visited in Jamaica where Bond clashes with crocodiles. Production construction noise has driven all the crocs and alligators to ground and Ross Kananga, the alligator specialist and handler, is busy digging them out of the mud where they have buried themselves. I have sent him word not to bother on my account.

Thursday, 2 November. B-Day Seventeen, and a day like any other on an 007 epic; tearing wings off aeroplanes, crashing cars and creating havoc at Lake Front Airport. The man responsible for many of the stunts is Joie Chitwood, who when he isn't breaking up planes for James Bond, tours the country with his team of stunt drivers in *The Greatest Show on Wheels*. There is no doubt in my mind that this Bond epic is going to be the most spectacular for its thrills and action. No credit to me. It is due to the General's careful planning and the excellence of the drivers, like Jerry Comeaux and Joie Chitwood.

There were angry mutterings today from some of the black stunt boys when Joie Chitwood's team, blacked up and bewigged, were chosen to stunt the spectacular skidding and crashing of planes and cars. It is understandable that Joie wanted his own boys but the black team were very angry and nobody is quite sure what will happen tomorrow.

A rather fragile, jaded little Miss Seymour came out to the location today to meet the unit. She arrived last night feeling bedraggled after a sixteen hour journey from London. She posed for Press pictures at Heathrow and when the clamour of cameramen dispersed discovered fog had delayed departure for two hours. There she was, a brand new star, all on her own and London Airport so packed she could not even get into the PanAm Clipper Club Lounge.

When she *did* arrive, having missed all her connections, Customs curiously counted her cases and concluded nobody needed all those clothes for an eight day visit. When she explained it was her wardrobe for the film, eyes lit up like jackpot signs on a pinball machine and they impounded every stitch. Harry Saltzman, who greeted her with Bollinger and a dazzling smile in her flower-filled room at the French Quarter Inn, spent a nervous night wondering how he was going to clothe his leading lady. It took the cunning Claude Hudson, our able Production Manager, to clear the confusion and claim her bags this morning.

For a leading lady to bring me a letter from her father-in-law is a new experience. She is married to Michael Attenborough, son of Richard, and when Dickie was in New York for the opening of *Young Winston* recently I dropped him a note. His reply said it was very sweet of me to offer to look after Jane, adding that he knew I would do this anyway. The letter continued: 'She is a delightful kid, bright, dedicated

44

and I might add, a bloody good little actress. Sheila [Dickie's wife] and I went up to Harrogate to see her Ophelia and I must say we were quite bowled over by her. She is, I fear, a little overtired in having not only to prepare for your picture but complete her work in *The Onedin Line*. I am sure Luisa will keep an eye on her for us. She may well need a shoulder to lean on.' Bang goes any lustful thoughts that might have been in 007's mind. Jane returns to London next week to finish off *The Onedin Line* series for BBC Television, where she was spotted by Harry and Cubby, and will rejoin us in Jamaica.

The President of United Artists, David Picker, and his wife, Joy, were here today. He is delighted by the few minutes footage he saw of *Live and Let Die* screened for him by Harry this morning. I was amazed to see him in the long location lunchtime queue with his wife, Harry and Jackie, one hundred and fifty crewmen, artists, stunt men and wives, waiting to be served on their plastic partitioned plates from the mobile catering truck. There is a democracy about American film units which I like. I never thought I would see the day when a film company President would queue with the crew and not pull rank.

In spite of our big brass from California, Harry still found time to corner me for cards in my caravan and siphon some more production money from me. I suppose I will go on playing with him until I find out how he cheats.

Friday. B-Day Eighteen. Disappear Diary. I'm too ill to talk.

Yesterday, my first day on set with my leading lady, Jane Seymour, and I ended up in hospital. It was nothing to do with the wild swing the script said she had to take at me. Rather more dreary than dramatic. It opened with a grim, grey morning and a drive to Lake Front Airport for further shots on the plane chase. We were shooting a scene where Bond has hailed a cab and finds that the driver is a villain in disguise. The cab doors lock and an unbreakable partition between him and the driver slides into place. I was sitting in the car when suddenly I felt grabbing pains in my lower regions. The sky got greyer and so did my complexion and Guy suggested I rest in my motor caravan. The pain got worse and by the time the unit broke for lunch I was more than ready for the First Assistant, Derek Cracknell's suggestion that a doctor be called. I did not need a diagnosis to tell me that my unromantic and uncomfortable kidney stones were acting up again. Harry insisted that a New Orleans specialist, Dr Wiener, was sent for. Dr Wiener arrived wielding a syringe of demarol which he shoved into my arm, informing Harry as he did so that work was out of the question for two hours. I began to feel woozy and nauseous and the doctor decided I was an emergency. I was rushed to Touro Hospital, New Orleans, in what must be the most elaborate and expensive ambulance the wide-eyed hospital orderlies had ever seen: my own elegant motor caravan which is big enough to carry a platoon of casualties.

Propped up in bed in the emergency ward I was drip-fed in the hope that pressure going through my kidneys could move the stones. I lay in a euphoric daze from the effects of the demarol with the drip needle in my arm when a strange young gentleman with swept black eyebrows started an interrogation. It began with:

'What's your name?' so I spelled my name out.

'Where do you live?' and I told him, Sherwood House. He said:

'Well, what's the street number?'

I said it didn't have a number. He said:

'Well, how do you get your mail?'

I told him the postman knows where I live.

'Well, where's that located?' he said.

46

'Buckinghamshire,' I said.

'Well, where's Buckinghamshire located?' he said.

'In England,' I said.

'Oh, well, what are you doing here?' he said.

I told him I was working.

'Oh, well, who are you working for?' he said.

I said Eon Films, the company name.

'And where are they?' he said.

I said I couldn't remember their address in New Orleans, and by that point I was having a hell of a job remembering who I was. I suppose he wanted all this information to make sure I could pay for my treatment, one of the less endearing habits of American hospitals, but before I could find out a friendly nurse rescued me and I was rolled off for an X-ray, to see what my stones were up to. Is there no end to all this posing for pictures, I ask myself.

The results five minutes later showed one little demon about to pop into the bladder and another had just exited the kidney. I spent another couple of hours in the hospital then Luisa arrived to take me back, rather shattered, to the hotel; in no state to address you, Dear Diary. Dinner at the hotel fell short of emergency service. It took an hour and a half for room service to arrive with a lukewarm and weary bowl of Gumbo soup, a local dish the contents of which I would hate to hazard a guess – cold lamb and tasteless vegetables. I could only attribute the slack service to the absence on holiday of our hotel host and owner, cheerful Charlie Slater.

I awoke this morning refreshed from a long restful night but if I was better the weather wasn't. The sky was black and heavy Louisiana rain lashed the windows while thirty miles away the unit was finishing the wedding party sequence in intermittent sunshine at Slidell. I breakfasted with my business manager, David Greenwood and his wife Phyllis, who arrived from London last night. Derek Coyte, the Publicity Director, and Jane joined us before leaving for a photographic session and I told her to take her biggest brolly and prettiest plastic dress.

I spent today close to the French Quarter Inn after my nasty bout of Friday. I took my children Geoffrey and Deborah to the local wax museum in the afternoon and learned that my favourite dice game, craps, was played originally by the French in New Orleans during the late eighteenth and early nineteenth centuries. The French were nicknamed 'Frogs' – *crapeaux* in French – hence craps. Information which will in no way help me win my next crap game.

On my return I came face to face for the first time with the villain of our piece, Yaphet Kotto, a mountain of a man; all six feet four and muscled two hundred and fifty pounds of him was waiting to meet me in the bar. I felt a bit of a beanpole by comparison. As Mr Big he has no scenes in New Orleans, but has come down for make-up tests. He may come out to Jamaica but we will be back in London for his first scenes.

Derek Coyte joined us and said as I had been on standby all Saturday how about doing a little work. A handful of journalists, he told me, who had stood in the drenching rain all day on the bayou without getting their interviews were waiting downstairs and he thought it would be 'convenient' for me to talk to them now. Convenient for them, no doubt. I am trying to think of new, bright, intelligent answers to the same questions. 'How is your Bond going to be different from Sean's Bond?' is the inevitable question, to which I inevitably reply, 'Well, he is he and I am me.' I get the feeling I always give the same interview; the same answers to the same questions.

Sunday, B-Day Nineteen and it is Guy Fawkes Day, in England, that is. At 9.30 A M I reckoned the only fireworks I was going to see would be when Harry came out on location to find that because of the light we had shot exactly nothing. We had been shivering out at Lake Front Airfield since what is laughingly called 'sun-up', but the only thing that came up at 6.30 AM were banks of grey clouds and a few belches from the crew; all suffering from last night's party hangovers. Ted Moore, Director of Photography, whose eyes I'm sure would have been bleary if I could have seen them, huddled his way into my trailer in search of warmth and a beer after a wine tasting party at Slidell.

By 10 AM a few streaks of sun filtered through and with its pallid beams bolstered by the brutes, the big arc lights powered by our own generators, we were able to get the cameras turning. Ted Moore came up with the real reason the light was bad. He says there are so many stills photographers snapping away that they are stealing all the light.

Today I got to say my second line of dialogue. But I speak only a few words before Jane, as Solitaire, takes a swing at me to distract the attention of my captors. This feint gives me the chance to dive under a parked jet plane and escape. Rehearsals for the running dive worked out well, and then they took the blankets away exposing gritty concrete.

My dive and roll took three attempts – or 'takes' in movie talk – and sorely grazed both my elbows and kneecap before the scene was in the can. The swing Jane should have swung the day I was rushed to hospital was shot today. It is her first full day on the picture and it reminds me of April Fools' Day, 1954, when as a budding young screen actor making my US debut in *The Last Time I Saw Paris* I had to throw a glass of Scotch in Van Johnson's face, punch him in the jaw and walk off with Liz Taylor. I was pretty bad. No wonder it took eighteen years for me to land 007.

Yaphet Kotto came out to visit the set today and towering over Jane and myself we lined up for pictures. The cameras clicked and suddenly I noticed frantic, pressing fingers become frenzied. I looked to learn why; Yaphet was punching the air with a black power salute. Whether he was serious or not I don't know but the sequel was a scorching row. Derek Coyte pointed out that the pictures would rouse resentment from the rabid whites and could be seen as an endorsement of black power by militant blacks. We are making anything but a political picture but Derek said the photographs syndicated far and wide would involve us in a controversy which could do nothing but harm. Yaphet was incensed. At midday he and the black stunt men lunched together and during the afternoon Derek Coyte was ostracized by blacks who had previously been pally.

Monday. B-Day Twenty. The same airfield location but what a difference today's bright sunshine made. The morale of the whole unit lifted with the clouds, and we moved along at a cracking pace. Ted Moore looked particularly pleased with life because there is nothing more distressing for the man directing photography – in cinematic slang the lighting man – than not having enough light to make his light meter needle move. The standard 'in' joke on location when the weather is dull is to ask the lighting cameraman if he wants a flashlight to read his meter.

We lined up for what, even on spectacular stunt terms, must be regarded as sensational. Many thousand pounds' worth of grounded D C3 passenger plane was parked on the airport apron. I buzzed about in the two-seater Cessna and the stunt began with a pursuing car missing me, hitting the tail of the Dakota and literally taking off to hurtle the full length of the passenger plane. Jim Heck's car, filmed by three visiting television teams, as well as our carefully placed cameras raced across a runway on to the apron, tipped the tail plane and took off. The watching crowd, sworn to silence, because we were shooting sound, could barely stifle a shout as the car flew the full length of the plane and crumpled into the wing. Jim Heck, who is as game as they come but had admitted he was scared of the stunt, stepped out shaken but unscathed.

Today was smash the aeroplanes day. One gone and at least another to go, possibly two. Film companies frequently think in terms of twos and threes in case the first crash of whatever is crashing goes wrong and the scene has to be reshot. Today was also the day Jimmy Bond literally had his wings clipped. As I was whizzing round Lake Front Airport in the two-seater Cessna with Mrs Bell, I whipped through half-closed hangar doors and the plane's wings were torn off leaving two foot stumps and flapping fabric on either side. The wings were sawn through to weaken them and off we went. If the stunt was not as dangerous as the the flying car and plane crash it looked just as effective. To see a plane disappear at speed into a hangar and emerge wingless the other side is an eye-opener. It worked so well the first time we shot it we did not have to wreck the reserve plane but it will never fly again. We had sawn through the wings in case it was needed. Anyone want to buy a plane with wobbly wings?

In the sequel shot I roared around the airport in the wingless plane, scattering the villains. The black stunt men who played them were among those who complained about the white stunt men blacking up yesterday. The trouble seems to have subsided today but last night they were on local television airing their grievances.

Shooting in New Orleans is nearly over and the first friendly face to leave was Tommy Lane, my companion of bayou boat chases. He called last night to say goodbye and we won't see him again until the next location in Jamaica. We are scheduled to fly there in six days' time if rain doesn't delay shooting further.

It is a month today since I arrived in New Orleans and I have become attached to the place. We know our way around the Quarter and we have our favourite restaurants. We are regulars at a little Chinese restaurant called Gin's with an unprepossessing exterior and marvellous food. Harry took us the first week we were here. We pay repeated visits there because the food doesn't pay repeated visits on us. Luisa and I are old hands at Chinese food and quite expert with chopsticks since visits we paid to Hong Kong and Singapore a few years ago en route to Australia. We were entertained to breakfast, lunch and dinner every day until Chinese food was coming out of our ears and Luisa was longing for a plate of spaghetti and I got twinges every time I thought of roast beef and yorkshire. Every course was served separately and between each dish a gin and tonic appeared. As the courses continued in perpetuity we were in danger of becoming severe alcoholics. The obligatory 'starter' is shark's fin soup and the host always dug me in the ribs with his chopsticks and said: 'Shark's fin soup velly good for "get it up".' Not only did Luisa get tired of it at every meal, she didn't think much of it as an aphrodisiac, either. Another upsetting Chinese habit for Luisa was when they pick a piece out of a dish with their chopsticks, taste it, put the rest back and then pass you a piece to taste from their own chopsticks. Not very hygienic.

Our first evening in Hong Kong, as a dozen of us congregated in the hotel lobby for dinner, I saw our host waving anxiously at a large voluptuous lady who was looming across the lobby. The next day when his wife had taken Luisa shopping and we were alone, he said: 'Yesterday you see lovely lady coming towards us in lobby?' I said I had and then he explained: 'I not sure your lovely Ruisa come with you, so I think I make assignation. Lovely lady in question have husband up liver and she very anxious for assignation, so when Ruisa and my honourable wife shopping another day maybe you have assignation?' I pointed out that I had neither the time nor the inclination.

*　　　*　　　*

B-Day Twenty-one and a seventy per cent chance of wet weather forecast. The clouds were heavy and pregnant with rain. A moist blanket of humidity hung over the airfield where we were shooting the plane chase. The mosquitoes were out in full force treating us all like Nick's Diner. By 8 AM we had the first shot in the can when down came the rain, so we moved our wingless two-seater Cessna inside the hangar to shoot the dialogue sequence between 007 and Mrs Bell while the electric storm raged around us. Ruth Kempf, who plays Mrs Bell delightfully, is a local actress who has never before played in a major movie.

Somebody up there must have heard Harry's prayers, for by lunchtime the heavens had cleared and after an al fresco lunch we moved off to – guess where? Slidell, to which I thought I had said a fond farewell. Rain caused the shooting schedule to be altered round and I was needed for one last bayou shot. This one really was the last of the bayous.

B-Day Twenty-two started off on a very black note when in the middle of my knees-bend morning work-out Mike Jones, my hairdresser, telephoned from London to tell me he would not be joining me in Jamaica as a unit hairdresser after all. Mike, who chopped off my locks for Bond, has been with me for several years but out of two hairdressers on the unit list it was decided to bring only one to Jamaica. Harry chose to axe my man which displeased me no end. I finished my work-out in a furious mood and flung my breakfast toast across the room in rage. Hairdressing might seem a hair-splitting issue to get so heated about but Mike, apart from being a thoroughly agreeable character, is highly competent and had been given, I believe, a clear understanding that he would link up with us on the Jamaican location.

I was still angry when we arrived at the New Orleans

International Airport location. In crazy back to front movie fashion, having already shot what happens to Bond after he gets to New Orleans, we filmed his arrival. The International Airport, in common with so many of the world's airports, is in the throes of extensive excavations and although we had permission from the airport authorities to film there, nobody cleared it with the construction teams. It posed production problems including parking. The unit drivers were really fed up; every time they found somewhere to park a chap in a hard hat came along and told them to leave.

We lunched, once more al fresco, in the backyard of a florist shop, where to welcome us the owners decked the tables with floral displays. It was a nice thought and the mosquitoes showed their appreciation by joining us.

After lunch we moved back to Lake Front Airport where Jane and I spent the afternoon in the back of a taxi while a glass partition bounced up and down like a back-handed guillotine between us and the driver until the scene was in the can. We were warned to keep out of the way of the partition because it came up with such speed it could take your fingers off in a flash.

Lighting inside the cab was tricky. From the outside the taxi looked like a giant lit-up meccano set with iron bars sticking out supporting lights aimed at the interior. The effect was a crazy car designer's dream; a motor which was mobile but with the headlights beaming on the back seat passengers. Balanced on the bonnet, like some mad motif, was the camera, aimed at us by Guy and Bob, both sprawled on their stomachs.

Work done I overheard an enlightening dinner time debate between my two children. The point at issue was which of them most resembled me.

Deborah said: 'I look like Daddy.'

Geoffrey said: 'Don't be silly. I look like Daddy.'

Deborah said: '*I* look like Daddy. Everybody says I look like Daddy, so I look like Daddy.'

Geoffrey, his temper a little more ragged, repeated through clenched teeth: 'I look like Daddy.'

Deborah decreed: 'I look like Daddy. You look like Mummy.'

Geoffrey settled it with his six-year-old steam-roller logic: 'How can you be like Daddy when your willy has got a a hole in it?'

B Day Twenty-three and a lovely day for a funeral. Back we went to the scene of the crime to continue the sequence which rain cut short. The sun dazzled the Docker Street scene in the heart of the French Quarter as the jazz men jostled for place in the procession. At the call for 'Action' the cortège, accompanied by beautiful black girls, strutted and sashayed under flower-decked sunshades to the Dixie-land beat of the band. The trouble was once they had started no one could stop them.

Derek Cracknell, First Assistant-Director, perched on the top of a ten foot high pair of steps, yelled 'Cut it' through his loud hailer. Drunk on the sound of Dixie they swayed on, then all broke into a dance. Watched by the crew and applauding crowd they writhed and rolled, their sunshades swaying like crazy cockatoos. Beaming, they stopped and were brought back to reality with a bump as Cracknell commented: 'If you think you've finished you're wrong. Back to positions, we're doing it again.'

After two more takes on the same scene Guy was happy and the dancers, with Jane Seymour swaying in the middle of them, were let loose off camera in a side street. The photo-graphers had a frantic few minutes at the sight of Jane letting her hair down with the dancers.

Photographers and the jazz funeral jogs my memory of an incident which occurred the first time we tried to shoot it. Harry was hurling abuse at anyone clutching a camera because they were in the way. He came across one man standing on a doorstep and told him to move on. The man said: 'Who are you?' 'This is my film,' said Harry. 'This is my house,' the man shot back.

Jane, David and I were not needed for the funeral scene so we sat around, as actors will, swapping tall stories on lines we have loved and loathed. I told them about a 'Saint' episode in which I had to say: 'He was responsible for perforating the intestinal tracks of Himmler's hatchet man with even more ulcers than bullets.' I was fine in rehearsal and just before the take the script girl bet me ten bob I would get it wrong. It was the worst thing she could have said. 'Take One. Action,' came the call and I went into 'He was responsible for per ... perf ... per ...' 'Cut!' came the shout. Fifteen takes later I ended up saying: 'He gave the Gestapo very nasty stomach ache.'

David and I were eventually called on set to play the scene where we enter the Fillet of Soul restaurant, a villains' hide-out, in search of Mr Big. The Art Department constructed the set overnight in front of a French Quarter Chinese laundry and had incorporated the real door of the shop into the plasterboard façade. David and I walked up to the restaurant with our best secret agent stroll and I made to open the door with Bond-smooth nonchalance, only to find the owner of the Chinese laundry had carefully locked it. We spent a nasty half-hour with everyone running around, including Harry, trying to get inside and get the door open. A small, but reluctant, crew member was delegated to shin a drainpipe and get through an open window but just then the owner came whistling down the street with the key in his pocket. These things never happen to the *real* James Bond.

Following the Fillet of Soul scene, Jane and I agreed to pose for pictures for Akhtar Hussein a photographer who was in something of a panic because he was leaving the following day and had not got the standard two shots of Jane and me together with me looking suitably protective pointing my gun. The problem was we had no gun. The twenty-five carried by our Property Department were fifteen miles away locked in a warehouse and by the time they could be brought over, the light in the French Quarter Inn courtyard where the session would be shot would have failed. David Dagley, who was covering for West Germany's *Bravo* magazine, desperately wanted a similar shot. Dan Slater was caught in the publicist's dilemma of having artists available on the one hand, photographers frantic for a specific shot on the other, but without indispensable props; in this case the gun.

The only gun in sight in the French Quarter was slung on the hip of a young point duty policeman and discussion revealed that, with his sergeant's permission, the policeman with typical Southern hospitality was quite happy to loan his gun on condition we borrowed him as well. After a street search the sergeant was found and gave the go-ahead. The policeman strolled into the French Quarter Inn courtyard smiling, took the bullets out of his Smith and Wesson .38 police special, which happens to be one of the guns I use in the picture, and sat down sipping coffee for half an hour watching while Jane and I worked with the photographers.

We have met with kindness from all branches of the Louisiana police, those from the local sheriff's office at Slidell, wearing their broad-brimmed Western hats, to the futuristic New Orleans City Force topped in spaceman-type helmets and one who even designed his own snappy uniform. Most have been friendly, but the custom-built cop was a bit too friendly for Jane when we were working at the airport where he was attached to us. He was constantly at her elbow trying to clinch a date. I still can't quite categorize him but he was some sort of special agent and had the kind of equipment, beginning with his own helicopter, which would make a British bobby's heart miss a beat. Apart from the statutory revolver, he carried a Mace gun and a belt clipped with bullet-sized pellets which he claimed were capable of almost anything but flying him to the moon. At the flick of a trigger one type of pellet flew from its small containing canister and covered the target in talcum powder. Another, again no larger than a lady's lipstick had a detachable head which became a ball of flame and flew 500 feet in the air. A third, the same size, contained a gas inflatable balloon which, triggered under water, would haul the holder to the surface.

B-Day Twenty-four the last day of shooting in New Orleans and oh, my head. I had a king-size hangover with varicose veins throbbing up and down the sides of my temples, and my brain felt like it was rolling around loose in my head like a pea in a drum, banging from side to side. We threw a cocktail party last night in the courtyard of our headquarters here in New Orleans to say thank you to the Mayor, Moon Landrieu, and other local dignitaries who have been such a help to us in making the film. A couple of the more colourful characters were John Mecom, who owns the New Orleans Saints football team, and a buxom blonde, lace-dressed lady who was introduced as the richest and most intelligent of the Texan millionairesses.

After lining my stomach with cocktails, David took Luisa, Jane and me off to the Maison Pierre for dinner. It was our first visit to this elegant restaurant where we were greeted by the owner's very attractive wife and an English head waiter from Coventry. It was a splendid evening with David and me polishing off three bottles of rather good wine, washed down with two cups each of Irish coffee. I can vaguely remember around midnight insisting that we go to a jazz club and Luisa's warning the only jazz I would hear would be her fist around my ear if I didn't come home this minute.

Today the location was the local railway station where Solitaire and Bond say goodbye to Felix Leiter. Because we could not get wardrobe and make-up vehicles into the station, the rendezvous point was the Hotel Pavillon where most of the crew are staying. David felt just as fragile as I did and we wandered over the hotel looking for the make-up room which turned out to be Paul Rabiger's bedroom. We found him slapping make-up on Jane with the remnants of his breakfast ham on a plate by the unmade bed. It was all too much at that time of the morning in my delicate condition, so David and I went on a fruitless Fernet Branca search to put us right. The hotel bar was opened up for us but their Fernet Branca bottle was empty. Our hopes rose as we strode to the station cocktail bar but that was closed.

A railway station is not the place to be with a hangover; the noise of departing trains does nothing to help the head. As I stood on the platform today gazing up into space I wished desperately it was Paddington and I could walk outside, get into my car and drive back to Denham. Despite the fact that Luisa and the children are here I still get desperately homesick. I miss things like an English cottage loaf, Golden Shred marmalade, the English papers with my morning tea. One is not demanding but they are the niceties of life.

I can't remember how many times I had to get on and off the train for takes and retakes on the farewell scene but I was beginning to feel like the guard. It wasn't helping my head either and by the time the cocktail bar was open I resembled Ray Milland's superb alcoholic performance in *Lost Weekend*. They didn't have Fernet Branca so we settled for a bloody mary and when I asked the waiter for the bill the barman said the manager had paid. Southern hospitality is no myth and nice things like this happen all over New Orleans.

We finished shooting just before one o'clock even though I mischievously tried to delay Guy simply because I knew he was itching to go off and swing a golf club with Ted Moore. Jane and I were kept busy into the afternoon by the photographers because she is leaving for London tomorrow where she has to finish off the *Onedin Line* before joining us in Jamaica.

Later in the afternoon I kept a dental appointment to find out how my fractured tooth was progressing. I am having electric treatment which is like testing if your toe is numb by hitting it with a hammer. First hit all the sensitive toes and when you get to the toe you can't feel when the hammer comes down they conclude it is numb. That is what they are doing with my teeth. I am now armed with enough antibiotics to go into business for myself. Should signs of an abscess appear I have strict instructions to dose up and whip off smartly for a root canal, which is a delusive dental term for taking the nerve out of the tooth. Ghastly!

Moving day in the movie business is a mammoth military operation. Two tons of equipment to be dismantled, crated and shipped to the airport for Customs clearance ready for the flight to Jamaica took the unit most of Saturday. Nobody felt much like it as they were all fragile from the effects of the farewell party our US crew had thrown the night before. From now on the crew will be British all the way. The rest of the English unit who have not been with us in the US will join us in Jamaica.

Luisa, Jane and I sensibly spent only an hour at the party before leaving to dine at the Rib Room in the Royal Orleans Hotel. Little did we know of the drama being played out at a neighbouring restaurant. Jane had accepted an invitation to a party that evening at Slidell before Harry asked her to join a dinner party he was throwing. Caught between two invitations she decided politically to join the Saltzmans and telephoned to say she would, after all, be able to join them. Jackie said the meal had already been ordered but she would see if another place could be added. Jane began to wish she hadn't called, but Jackie said she would call back and confirm. It slipped Jackie's mind so Jane spent the evening with us and Harry sat with a vacant seat to his left, fuming about actresses not showing up.

The bouillabaisse carefully ordered for 9 PM appeared at 11 PM, and the only resemblance to the traditional French dish was its name. It was preceded by a salad, 'to clean the palate which is the way they do it in France,' informed the waiter. This was too much for Harry who lived for years in France and is not at his most patient in restaurants at the best of times. He exploded. The whole restaurant learned that it was not the custom in France to clean the palate with salad and they had not been served with anything to soil their palates with. The little fall out Harry and I had is still bubbling merrily away. We are polite to each other and that is all, so I was not at the repast.

The weather turned suddenly colder today but the chill in the air warmed under the sunny smile of Gloria Hendry whose entry into the French Quarter Inn courtyard was straight out of a Bond movie. I can't remember what colour her dress was; I only know it fitted just below her coffee-coloured skin and when she walked part of her seemed to move in the opposite direction. The overall effect is – wow! She is to play Rosie Carver, a double agent bedded by Bond. It was our first meeting and she joined Jane, Harry and me for coffee. Jane was leaving almost immediately for London. Ah, well. Off with the old and on with the new.

The rest of the day proved to be just as interesting, if in a different way. Jim Garrison, the District Attorney of New Orleans, who conducted his own investigation into the assassination of Kennedy, invited me, along with a couple of FBI agents, to his office to view some film. I am not at liberty to disclose what I saw but it left no doubt in my mind that it was not Oswald who fired the fatal shot. Garrison's assertion is that Oswald was not acting alone but as part of a CIA conspiracy. An interesting conclusion to 007's five weeks in Louisiana.

*   *   *

The French Quarter Inn at 7 A M was astir with the sounds and excitements of departure as we gathered for the last time in the dining-room. The gathering had a holiday air as if we were all going on a jet age trip to the surf-side. End of term pranks seemed in order. I telephoned Derek Coyte, disguising my voice, and said I was Herb Weintrap of AP for one final interview with Roger Moore, and even the unit drivers, on their last mission for us, caught the spirit. One of them put the story round that Harry, dazzling in a matching cream 'Godfather' suit and hat, was hopping mad because someone had tipped coffee over him. Their disappointment was visible when Harry walked out stain-free and creamier than cream.

Our Boeing 727 Eastern Airlines charter waited in the freight area of New Orleans International Airport. It took forever to load the luggage and we had so much some of it had to go in the cabin toilet. Had there been excess baggage charges it would have been cheaper to buy the plane. Guy spent the time before take-off practising his golf swing on the fringe of a field flanking the apron while the rest of us gathered in groups for family album photos, until it was time to board for the two and a half hour flight to Jamaica, which doubles for Dr Kananga's deadly island of San Monique. No sooner were we seated than Harry had his fifty-two little friends spread across the pull down tray which was a bit strong, and I discovered flying charter is not always cheapest. Flying over Cuba a champagne brunch was served and the party atmosphere prolonged as people sipped and seat-hopped until we landed in Montego Bay to searing heat and a calypso welcome from a steel band.

Before setting off on the two hour drive to Ocho Rios, lunch was served at the Iron Shore Golf Club much to Guy's delight. He and Ted Moore made straight for the links while the rest of us enjoyed a delicious meal on the open terrace. On the drive to the club I was bugged by the local Press whose chief interest was how much money I was getting.

'I don't discuss money; only with my bank manager, agent and tax man,' I told them.

'But we heard you were getting a million dollars,' one persisted.

'Then why ask?' I rejoined.

'Would it be right to assume that is what you are getting?' he asked.

'If you wish to assume that it is your privilege,' I answered.

'Then what are you getting?' he demanded.

'I don't discuss money . . .' It went on like that until we got to the club where I was able to shake them.

The winding road by the blue Caribbean through waving palms and sugar cane plantations took us past Discovery Bay, where Columbus landed, and on to Ocho Rios and the Sans Souci Hotel, our home for the next two weeks. New Orleans seemed far away and this was another world. I have never been a city lover; in spite of the charm of the French Quarter Inn, its picturesque setting and everything New Orleans has to offer, this is the place for me.

From the terrace of our two bedroomed split-level apartment set in the hillside I can hear the limpid Caribbean waters below lapping the pink terracotta walls. Terraced walks surround two azure swimming pools and tropical flowers of every hue peek out of the palm fronds and lush green vegetation. Multi-coloured birds, competing with the flowers for beauty, chirp cheerfully; and why not? They know they are living in Paradise.

Monday was a rest day in Paradise. A whole day with not even a photographer to remind me of Bond.

The *Daily Gleaner* reported our arrival in Jamaica in this morning's paper with a few glaring inaccuracies, the best being a reference to the 'tour director' Mr Henry Saltzman. Well, I said the flight over had a holiday air.

Work begins again tomorrow.

Back to work, B-Day Twenty-five, and our first location in Jamaica was a small silver crescent of sand at the foot of a steep cliff. Had I not known the crew was all British now, I would have guessed when I arrived on location this morning at 7.45. Tables, neatly cloth-covered, lined the roadside and the crew to a man were drinking tea. That's the English for you; everything stops for a cup of char and they are prepared to go to any lengths to get it. The carpenters had dropped a rope down the cliff from tree to tree to help people up and down and about mid-morning, before my incredulous gaze, down the rope like a one-armed fiddler came Colin Davidson, the clapper/loader, juggling a tin tray full of teacups.

We have a new member of the cast today who has just arrived in Jamaica and is suffering badly from the heat. Strange really, because he is Jamaican-born, Roy Stewart, who is playing Quarrel. Maybe it is because he has to wear a black rubber diving suit all day. Still, as I told him, it's a good way to lose weight. This is his first visit to Jamaica for twenty years and, not surpringly, he notices a few changes.

My home-on-wheels was left behind in New Orleans and I miss it sorely. The only trailer the production office could find here has a toilet that doesn't work; so I am the proud possessor of a rather nice green bucket. I don't have so many visitors now I have no stove to brew up, either.

We returned to the Sans Souci this afternoon to shoot scenes around the hotel lobby and shops. Holiday makers from as far afield as Newcastle-on-Tyne to Chicago staying at neighbouring hotels were enlisted as extras to dress up the background. They sat around under the blazing sun watching the cameras set-up. Even with a brilliant lighting man like Ted Moore it takes time to place lights and reflector boards in the proper positions, especially when photographing a face as old and tired as mine! The ninety degree heat began to take its toll and they did what seemed to them the most natural thing in the world and ordered drinks all round. Harry saw what was happening and jumping up and down, absolutely irate, screamed at Claude Hudson, the Production Supervisor, that he wasn't paying people to sit around getting drunk while we were all working. I didn't envy Claude's job explaining to the holiday makers they must not drink on the set. Somehow I don't think he tried.

As they sat sipping their forbidden drinks, photographer John Bryson, a big, craggy, moustachioed man, moved among them on a mission some might consider the most enviable in the world but to me far from it. With a profuse amount of perspiration plopping from his sunburnt brow he picked with practised observance the prettiest girls in the crowd. Then, keeping an eye open for husband or boy-friend in the background, for all the world like the proverbial dirty old man, chatted them up to pose for *Playboy*. And we all know what that means. Big John, as I have christened him, a leading light among American photographers, is attached to the unit as a special photographer and his *Playboy* spread is just one of those he will do on *Live and Let Die*.

Whenever we shoot a crowd scene it is his task to talk the loveliest girls into posing in the nude. He had great success in the New Orleans jazz funeral scene with a strikingly beautiful black girl he spotted. She is a twenty-year-old, still at college, and with her mother's permission and *x* amount of dollars, she happily posed. I have not seen the pictures yet but John tells me I will never believe the shape of this beauty.

John is sharing one of the lush apartments here with Derek Coyte and we have dubbed them 'the Odd Couple' after being regaled with their hair-raising domestic experience. They have constant tests of one-upmanship and John's latest is to get me to scream bloody murder at Derek, who has final responsibility for photography, because John has propositioned Luisa to appear in *Playboy* and she is furious about it.

Shooting was over early and I was able to join Luisa and the children by the pool for the afternoon, but by 5 PM, when the sun had dropped down with tropical swiftness, we were ready to shoot again. It was a night sequence where Bond makes his first entrance into the hotel and learns that a mysterious 'Mrs Bond' has already checked in.

Even when filming inside the Sans Souci grounds we attracted the inevitable rubber necks. The last thing I would want to encounter on holiday is a film unit and I often wonder how they would like a bunch of actors gawping at them while they counted money in a bank or turned out a tricky piece of machinery on a lathe. I wonder, too, if they would always smile and appear eager to have their snaps taken while clutched in the arms of somebody's fat wife. Would they mind a demand for an autograph on a tiny piece of toilet paper or the silver paper from a cigarette packet with a pen, which, if one is produced, doesn't write.

I have been asked to sign all sorts of strange things including hands, arms and actual breasts. I remember Danny Kaye, coming over on the plane, was asked to sign a stewardess's blouse in a protuberant place. My nastiest moment with autograph hunters was years ago when I was making *Ivanhoe*. I stepped from a car at the stage door where a mob of teenagers surrounded me with autograph requests. I was smoking a cigarette and to have both hands free I stuck it in my mouth. Suddenly a teenage cockney voice said: ''ere mate, let's 'ave a souvenir,' and my cigarette was pulled out of my mouth taking a lump of lip with it. At the same time I felt a button go and a hand on my fly. My proudest possession was about to be produced for public examination. I hollered and fled.

Tomorrow Guy has banned all visitors because the voluptuous Gloria Hendry and I are going to play our love scene and he wants a closed set in order to concentrate. *He* wants to concentrate! Luisa, knowing tomorrow is my love scene with Gloria, has been plying me with questions all evening.

'You do love *me*, Roger, don't you?' she asked.

'Of course, I do,' I replied. 'I shall just be doing a job. It's my work.'

'Yes. I know,' sighed Luisa and, lapsing into Italian, said '*Non voglio che hai piacere nel lavorare.*' Literally translated, 'Don't enjoy your work too much.'

B-Day Twenty-six and I was wide awake before six, studied my lines for the day, then took off for the swimming pool to do my physical jerks. I was not there first. Creasing the pool with a rhythmic crawl was the lovely Gloria. She must have thought I was raving mad with my running, toe touching and knee-bends. She left and I bid her a cheerful goodbye as she needs more time in make-up than me and I repaired to my apartment for two three-minute eggs before leaving for the location and the love scene. The setting was extraordinarily beautiful with a backdrop of cascading water. My trailer was inhabited by Paul, the make-up man, who was busy on Gloria; a process which can only be described as gilding the lily. I wandered out into the bright sunshine where the crew were brutalizing their eggs and bacon. Harry was alarmed to see they were eating off china plates and asked what happened to the plastic ones like we used in Louisiana.

After a quick polish with Paul's make-up sponge to reduce my tan I was ready. The tan has to be subdued because in four weeks or so we shall be shooting at Pinewood Studios in breezy, wet Buckinghamshire. My tan will start fading away in the fog which could present a skin colour continuity problem, unless it is controlled.

Half a mile up a hill-side our props for the love scene

were ready. It was to take place during a picnic and blankets and a table-cloth were laid out and the set cleared and closed. Except for John Bryson and the unit stills man, George Whitear, photographers were barred, so when we saw a long lens peeping through the palms there was near panic. Vic Heutschy, the American publicist, set off to sort it out. He found himself explaining to some unsuspecting American tourist who had been aiming his lens at a bird that photography was forbidden. The bewildered gentleman found it difficult to believe because the property had been advertised as public. Acquainted with the circumstances he showed a decided disinterest in Gloria's glistening charms and flew off to photograph the feathered variety.

So Gloria and I got busy. I will not bore you with the details except to say that she put her heart, body and soul into her work. For further illustration you could always, of course, see the film.

Shooting on location today really took it out of the crew, especially the sparks. Sometimes in a studio you get short-tempered with the ETU types, that is Britain's Electrical Trades Union, who threaten to pull the plugs out and stop the world going round unless they get their way. Here they really have to work. Today, to light the hill-side set, they were lugging hundreds of yards of cables and heavy lamps in ninety degree heat. I put myself in a plastic suit for half an hour every morning to sweat and they sweat for ten or twelve hours. Our second location was some two hundred yards higher so they had to start cabling again. It was not possible in time for more shooting today so we finished work at 3.30.

Speculation on what happens after love scenes on film sets I believe is rife. Do they continue in private or do they stand up and slap each other? The truth is much more mundane, and usually along the lines of what happened to Gloria and me today. We shared a car for the drive back to the Sans Souci and chatted about everything under the sun, except what had happened earlier.

B-Day Twenty-seven. 5.30 AM and I staggered out into the dark for forty minutes of gymnastics feeling friendly with the world at large which was more luck than management because last night I invited a hangover. We had a long, leisurely dinner in the elegant air-conditioned dining-room at the Sans Souci in the convivial company of the First Assistant, Derek Cracknell and his actress wife, Julie. With us was Geraldine, my secretary and tutor to Geoffrey and Deborah, and Doree Schneider of the Schneiders of Slidell who has come to Jamaica as a jet age camp follower.

Anyway, I enjoyed my tipple and I was thinking as I worked my way through my physical jerks this morning how my drinking habits change from country to country. Here it is rum, I suppose because I lace it with lime and my sub-conscious says the vitamin C keeps away scurvy, Mutiny on the Bounty-style. In America I renew my jolly acquaintance with Jack Daniels (Bourbon whisky), in England I drink Scotch and in Italy white wine.

My early morning loving mood embraced Luisa and I prepared a quick quiet breakfast myself instead of turfing her out of bed. I made my own tea and if I do pat myself on the back I am always pleased by the way I brew it. I like it strong; my favourite is Army tea, there is nothing like it. Made in any sort of receptacle, like a scrubbed out oil drum stuck on an open fire, two pounds of tea, two pounds of sugar and four cans of Carnation milk poured in and left to bubble, with a twig stuck on top to collect the soot and ashes. That is real tea but what Luisa would think if I lit an open fire on the terrace of our penthouse and began brewing up I shudder to think.

I did not drive to the location this morning with Harry as I sometimes do; he was locked in one of his daily two hour calls to London, New York and California. He really can't live without a telephone and phones you from the ends of the earth at four in the morning to ask you what's new.

We were shooting the sequence where Rosie is executed.

Poor little Gloria, barefooted and wearing one of my vests and nothing else, literally tripped her way through the undergrowth until she runs backwards on to one of Mr Big's bullets. I followed in hot pursuit to find her still warm body lying on the grass being eaten by ants, much to Gloria's disgust. My immediate reaction is what a terrible waste. She looks very good and will do for a lot more years to come and Mr Big is a fool to shoot her.

From there we moved back to the water. This time the sea. Our boating base is a jetty which juts from a silver sand beach five miles from the Sans Souci. There was one of our aquajet boats by the jetty and I needed no encouragement to leap in and take Gloria for a spin with George Whitear, our stills photographer. I was concentrating on the driving and deliberately causing as much spray as I could to cool us off when I glanced over my shoulder to see Gloria without her towelling robe, or anything else for that matter. Her arms were outstretched skywards over the stern and George was snapping happily away. All I needed was for Luisa to be sitting on the beach with binoculars and she would have had my guts for spaghetti.

Our spin was short-lived and I was called back through the walkie-talkie I took with me to shoot on Quarrel's twenty-eight foot cruiser. Quarrel, as Bond aficionados will recall, is the man who helped Bond in *Doctor No*, and is played by Roy Stewart. We rehearsed on the boat for forty minutes and it was lunch time. George Crawford, who has joined us from London with his location catering services, had spread out his tables and cloths and we tucked in to a tasty repast. Cold chicken, cold beef, chutney and some scorching, local, hot pepper sauce and a couple of glasses of milk. After that, two halves of pears in heavy syrup, and I was in no mood to work as we chugged to sea in dazzling sunshine.

Luckily I was not in the first shot and although there was not much room to hide from the camera's all-seeing eye

70

I did find a corner and the swell of the sea soon rolled me into a sound sleep. I was rudely awakened by the General who suggested I sleep somewhere else because my backside was in the picture. Why I called Guy the General I am not sure because he is in fact a former Royal Navy Officer and he was in his element with our sea shooting.

Steaming two hundred yards to our starboard was an armed Jamaican Navy coastal patrol boat which has been seconded to us as our service boat. It carries the members of our crew not needed on Quarrel's boat, a much smaller craft, as well as lights and a foredeck full of our equipment.

The Captain of the patrol boat suddenly sighted a naked man aboard a yacht and turned off to see what was going on. He cruised quietly alongside and found the man sound asleep on his cabin roof. The Captain bellowed through his loud hailer and asked him where he had cleared Customs and where he was bound for. The lone yachtsman, who was absolutely starkers, sprang behind a somewhat slim mast to try and hide his embarrassment, while our unit nurse snapped pictures either for her private collection or *Cosmopolitan*.

Friday. B-Day Twenty-eight. The alarm turfed me out of bed in a black mood. Luisa was not talking to me; snoring but not talking. The night before we had dined with the Pringles; Ian Pringle, one of the owners of the Sans Souci Hotel who has vast interests on the island, is Jamaican born of Scottish descent and his family have lived here for two hundred years. He has done a splendid job with the Sans Souci.

The whole ten acre complex is the vision of this pleasant, soft-spoken, English-educated gentleman. The entire hotel area had to be literally chiselled out of the cliff side and has a fourteen foot retaining wall, which Ian calls 'the great wall of China.' The buildings are mellow and merge with the landscape as if they were built centuries ago instead of only last year. One of the secrets is the nursery he hired to grow and nurture the plants and shrubs while the hotel was undergoing construction so that when it was finally finished the flowering foliage was transplanted, to burst into bloom and hide the scars of excavation. His dream, built on wind, sand and stars, has become a tropical truth of beauty. He has indeed created a paradise.

While gathering for pre-dinner drinks Derek Coyte had asked me to have pictures taken with one of the girls John Bryson found for *Playboy* and Luisa got needled at my interrupting dinner to go off and do photographs. Perhaps she thought as they were for *Playboy* the girl would start flashing her mamillaries at me and I would be tempted; but being a nice, normal 007 of course I wouldn't be. I made myself more unpopular at table by saying: 'I just thought I would mention, dear, that I am out of limes to mix my rum punches.'

'Mention eet to your secretary,' replied Luisa, loftily.

When I came down for breakfast this morning with the black freeze on to discover we were out of eggs I was tempted to go up and tell La Bella Luisa that I didn't want to wake my secretary but would she mention the fact there were no eggs for my breakfast.

In a highly liverish mood I went to look for my driver and found Harry; a bunch of car keys in his hand instead of the usual deck of cards and he drove me out to the location. Harry had not been out to this location before and I had. We sped at sixty miles an hour round hairpin bends and I was saying: 'Turn right here, Harry,' and he was saying, 'No, not here,' and finally we finished up going round a fenced-in hotel car park half a dozen times before he admitted defeat and said: 'All right, where's the location?'

We bumped our way over a grass track to my trailer where my liverish feeling was not helped by the smell of the cheese omelette Gloria was noshing her way through while having her make-up done. By 7.15 anchors were up and we were away on Quarrel's boat again. The sequence was where Rosie Carver thinks that Quarrel is out to kill Bond and comes to the rescue in a minuscule bikini clutching a large revolver.

The sea was calm when we began but as the morning went on it got rougher and rougher and poor Roy Stewart, still complaining about the heat of his homeland, was going greener than the tropical vegetation. We tried to cheer him up with chats about fried bacon and eggs and tripe and onions, which turned his green a paler shade of yellow. It is funny what suggestion can do. More years ago than I care to remember my mother and I saw a film with a comedy scene where a cook aboard a boat in a raging Atlantic storm was trying to make a pork stew. As the boat rolled he chased a large piece of fatty pork all over the galley trying to plop it into a pot slopping over with half-cooked carrots and onions. I heard choking sounds at my side and there was my mother being violently sick. It was the first time I had ever known anyone to be sea sick in the cinema.

When it was time for tea Derek Cracknell called our escorting Jamaican Naval vessel on the short wave radio and with a hard to port the Jamaican Navy brought George Crawford alongside with his Neptune Catering Services; an urn of tea, an urn of coffee and a lot of sticky buns.

The sea was so rough I thought we were going to swing to our tea by breeches buoy but with deft navigation and a dozen fend-offs we transferred to the larger vessel. Commander Hamilton, as I call him at sea, soon had us back for another choppy two hours before finishing the sequence and returning inside the coral reef to the calm of the harbour.

Once inside the reef I threw off my denims I wear for the scene and clad in my shorts swam the last few yards to shore. I made lunch before anybody and got first pick of the cold chicken. There was no lounging about after lunch. We set off to sea again leaving behind the luncheon table set on a silver beach beneath straw umbrellas. It is criminal to work in these conditions and I cannot help but envy the happy holiday makers having a wonderful time who, in turn, imagine we are having a wonderful time, too. In a way we are, but work is work no matter where in the world you are doing it.

Heavy rain clouds slowed us down in the afternoon and we chugged up and down for an hour waiting for a patch of sunshine. Yesterday we had used some mullet as a prop and it had inadvertently been left on board. It was beginning to hum a bit and we passed the time throwing it over the side to attract the sharks who, with admirable taste, ignored it. Eventually the sun shone through and we completed the shot, returning to shore at 4 o'clock. By 4.30 PM I was poised on the lower terrace of the Sans Souci before the welcoming warm waters of the bay. I plunged and wished I hadn't. Nobody had bothered to tell me the water there is only three feet deep.

B-Day Twenty-nine and from our vantage point at sea the golden minarets and white towers of Solitaire's house atop a two hundred foot cliff etched a sky ribboned with rainbows. The rainbows were real; the warm rain was real, but the house, a suitably strange abode for our mystic heroine, was just the plasterboard creation of our Art Department. From our boat it looked as though a giant hand had painted the scene and framed it with heavy green foliage and darkened clouds.

The cool breeze, whipping up the blue waters and turning them grey-green, had come as a blessing from the heat. When the first ponderous drops of tropical rain fell, twenty-three of us huddled in the cabin and coach-house of Quarrel's boat to sit out the storm. 'Chalky' Props revealed a hidden talent when he produced a mouth organ and within minutes a Saturday night at the local type sing-song was under way. As the boat rolled and tropical rain tattooed on

74

the roof the gorgeous Gloria regaled us with a heart-rending version of 'Summertime'. As quickly as it came the storm moved on; away went Chalky's mouth organ and out came the camera.

After lunch we cruised ten miles down the coast to a lovely lagoon where we worked until 4 PM. I returned to the Sans Souci to unnerving news. My son, Geoffrey, had been rushed to hospital with distended stomach and abdominal cramps. The local doctor's diagnosis of abdominal restrictions, twisted gut and gastro-enteritis was enough to drive a doting mother to distraction and Luisa was more in need of treatment than Geoffrey, who was actually suffering from a little gas brought on by constipation and too much swimming.

The incident recalled my childhood when, as an overweight ten-year-old with bellyache, my panic-stricken mother took me on an 88 bus to Westminster Hospital Casualty Department. There, the doctor, stethoscope dangling, pressed well scrubbed fingers across my abdomen then invited twenty medical students to do the same. I was heaved on my side and the students took it in turns to examine my rear end and agree on acute appendicitis. There was not a bed to be had in the hospital so I was rushed by ambulance to St Giles Hospital in Camberwell with my mother holding one hand and a nurse taking the pulse of the other. A doctor there put his finger on the trouble, so to speak; not acute appendicitis but acute constipation. Like father, like son. Geoffrey, just as I had all those years ago, had to suffer the indignity of an enema and was soon completely recovered.

This evening was a very relaxed affair for the whole unit because tomorrow is Sunday and a rest day. The best way to relax in the tropics is to gaze through the bottom of a tall glass that seconds before contained rum and fruit juices. About ten of us staggered down to a place called the Little Pub. Nothing like an English local. It is a Caribbean calypso club built of bamboo with tropical bushes between the tables. A straw roof covers the restaurant while dancers writhe in the open air heavy with smells of blossom, rum and sweat. The evening ended down the road at another club, The Ruin, where we watched lithe limbo dancers snake under a burning horizontal bar. Rum had readied us for a crack at Calypso dancing; then more rum and we were ready for bed.

Sunday, rest day and a nothing to do day. At lunch I had a couple of hairs of the various dogs and began to feel better until Harry came along and led me like the proverbial gambolling lamb to the card table. The afternoon was sunny and satisfying. Guy came with the good news that he had seen the rushes, not the green riverside variety but the film back from processing, showing my love and long dialogue scene with Gloria and he was extremely pleased.

As the sun was setting over the silhouetted palms the phone rang and my agent, Dennis Van Thal, told me from London that he had on my behalf politely bowed out of the two million dollar production *Getting Rid of Mr Straker*. It is a film Mel Frank and I planned before I knew I was to be Bond and starred Lee Remick, Orson Welles, Terry-Thomas and David Hedison. It has a hilarious script written by Mel Frank, Michael Pertwee and Jack Rose. I should have played the part of a private detective who wants to join MI5 but as he can't shoot straight, suffers from hay fever, sea sickness, vertigo and a fear of fast cars he hasn't a hope. Playing a bumbling secret agent between two straight Bond films would not do the 007 image any good so I reluctantly decided against it. But what a lovely position for a struggling actor to be in, I thought, to be able to turn down two million dollar productions willy nilly.

*   *   *

Monday, B-Day Thirty. Today we began shooting a far-out feature of the film, the kite flying sequence. To gain access to Solitaire's guarded cliff-top home Jimmy Bond is harnessed in a sixteen foot delta wing kite which takes off after being towed by a speed-boat. Easier said than done, for the one thing kite flyers need is wind from the right direction, and not too much of it.

Bill Bennett, the Australian Orville Wright of the kite set, has been brought over from England to show me the ropes. He designed his kites after a lot of trial and error when he came across a sail configuration drawn by Leonardo da Vinci. Flying over two miles at a height of 800 feet along the coast and landing on the jagged cliffs beside Solitaire's house is no joke and I hope Leonardo got his drawing right. Ours is a sea take-off but Bill says it can be done from snow slopes or from behind cars, boats or even motor cycles.

For the close-ups I am harnessed in the kite which is suspended from a hundred-foot-high crane perched on the cliff-top. The crane swings the kite over the cliff-edge and the shot shows me kicking an unsuspecting black guard over the edge before I land.

We began shooting before sun-up hoping the wind would be in the right direction, but by 9 AM it was whistling fiercely around the 400 foot cliff and the vultures were hovering hopefully in case we were crazy enough to try and fly. We were beaten and went back to a boat scene for the rest of the day.

Today I was on stand-by and tonight Harry took about thirty of us, including five children, to a reggae concert. We met in the Casanova Restaurant for dinner before the concert's 8.15 start. At 7.30, just as our first forkfuls were poised to go into our mouths, one of the island's frequent power cuts plunged the room into blackout. If the hotel lights were out it was a safe bet they were out at the concert hall three miles down the road and a driver was hastily dispatched to report. An hour passed while the children ran about, Deborah with her fourteen left feet fell over and hurt her hip, tears were wiped away, the children got restless and kept asking when we were going. Then, like a miracle, the lights sprung on at 9 o'clock to a resounding cheer. It was a bit like the twopenny rush at Saturday morning pictures and off we all went in a charabanc hired for the occasion.

Outside the theatre hordes of people thronged the approach as our bus ploughed its way through to the entrance and we all disembarked. 'Everybody stick close to me,' shouted Harry, forging through the resentful mob. I clasped my son in my arms and we heaved our way through the narrow, open door into the open-roofed concert hall where the two front rows of hard little seats had been reserved for us. Our party was allowed in first and sat for thirty minutes watching a youthful audience squeeze through a single door one at a time while a stern faced expert frisked them for flick knives and an armed policeman stood by.

Half an hour passed and the audience, some high on the local ganja or marijuana, began to get restless. At last a number of gentlemen came on the three foot of stage in front of a cinema screen and began to set up instruments and I realized to my horror that we were faced with, not an evening of folk dancing as Harry had thought, but a pop concert. The crowd's mood, marked first by cheerful chatter, became a dull ominous drone of discontent, and by the time the show finally began they were riotously restless.

A large, fat, sweaty gentleman, very drunk, announced to the crowd who could not have cared less that the star of *Live and Let Die*, the new James Bond, was in the audience. While I hung my head miserably dreading the inevitable bow I must take, he went on to say the producer, the director and the cast were also present.

78

The show did not improve with the advent of a large lady singer in bright blue who had to wrestle with the fat gentleman for possession of the microphone, missing her twelve bar intro in the process. Three men came on and removed the now paralytic MC. We left at the first opportunity, filing out smartly, carrying our sleepy children and took our coach back to the Sans Souci.

B-Day Thirty-one. I was turfed out of bed this morning by the persistent ringing of the telephone. It was one of the assistants telling me my 'stand-by' call had changed to a 'get-there' call. Paul Rabiger and Colin Jamison, the hairdresser, were pounding at the door and before I could get my three-minute egg down Paul attacked me with a make-up sponge and Colin combed knots from my hair. Dressed in my costume I was hustled up to the cliff-top for a kite flying shot. But we weren't quick enough; the wind was up and the kite was down.

Instead I talked to a charming lady from *Woman's Own*, Iris Burton, and if it was not the most in-depth interview I have given on this picture it was one of the most enjoyable. The question that still rolls at me as relentlessly as the camera is: 'How is your Bond going to be different from Sean Connery's Bond?' I am absolutely fed up with being asked that and I have, at last, thought of an answer. I will ask writers how their column is going to be different from everybody else's column.

Today was long, hot and gruelling. I was bounced about on the end of a kite hovering over the edge of a cliff. Landing on a square of tissue paper is not that difficult in itself but try looking nonchalant while you are doing it!

While I was careering over the cliff edge there was an even more dangerous drama unfolding among the Jamaican crowd of spectators which had collected in the coconut trees three hundred yards from where we were shooting. How it began is anybody's guess. It could have been a chance remark or a further round in an old feud. They had been standing there for five hours, the sun was searing and bottles of beer had been handed round. Suddenly there was a shout, two men broke from a mêlée, one raining blows on the other. Two others set on the winner who ran like hell across a field and a third turned on the girl-friend of the man who had bolted. She drew a knife and stood with her back to a bush. Several voices from the crowd called 'drop it' then a man produced an axe from somewhere and did a kind of war dance in front of her. The girl, looking terrified, held on to her knife. By then the girl and part of the crowd were in camera shot and Nick Hippisley-Coxe, one of the assistants, quite oblivious to the drama, strode through them telling them to stand back. Amazingly, they did. The girl picked up her handbag, put the knife in it, the axe disappeared and the crowd dispersed.

After the day's work I got back to the hotel hot, sticky and tired and ran straight into trouble. David Steen, a freelance photographer I have known for some years who joined us in New Orleans, asked me to do a still with Gloria and I posing as a bride and groom to be captioned Mr & Mrs Bond. David got the idea after a scene in which Bond checks into the hotel and finds Gloria, as Rosie Carver, has bluffed her way into his bungalow by posing as Mrs Bond. I knew if I traipsed all the way down to my apartment to tell Luisa I was home but was going out again to do a still, she would say what the hell was I going to do a still for when I had finished work? I would say the still was important and she would say so are we. Rather than face all that I sat myself down on the top terrace to wait for Gloria to appear. Luisa appeared instead and said: 'Is it too much for you to come and say good evening?'

I was stung to reply: 'It is too much when you are tired.'

She disappeared in a huff to be replaced by Gloria in virginal white clutching a bouquet with her large diamond ring reversed as a wedding ring. With me in elegant black, we posed arm in arm for the picture. A man has got to do what he has got to do.

Luisa was not the only one ready to tell my fortune. Somewhere on the lower seaside terrace was the black obeah, Doctor David Hinds, who, among other claims to fame, has served nine months in a Jamaican gaol for witchcraft. As *Live and Let Die* has a voodoo background and tell-tale tarot cards are a linking device in the picture, the publicity people thought it would be jolly if I had my fortune told and the procedure televised.

The sun had dipped below the sea as Doctor Hinds and I sat in a summer house illuminated by Ted Moore's lights. Turbaned and backed by five incanting obeah students, he began. Chris Doll's camera rolled, and I learned within the next year or so I shall have an operation for what he thought would be gall stones. Slightly ruffled because, as I have mentioned, I suffer from kidney stones, so he could have been on the right track, I sat up to hear him say that I would be going to the Far East, perhaps Tibet, during the next three years. Harry could hardly have confided the fact that the next Bond, *The Man With the Golden Gun* will be made in Bangkok. Turning over his tarot cards, he told me that I was going to have a car accident in an Oldsmobile in which I would suffer some brain damage and when I gave him a bewildered blink he added with a happy smile that it would not be fatal. He finished on a fact about 'my son or adopted son' and must have meant Geoffrey. My son it seems will be a prominent parliamentarian. When I asked Geoffrey tonight if he wanted to be Prime Minister of England, he said 'Yes', which must be the shortest acceptance speech on record. Then he added he'd rather be James Bond.

Andrew Michelin, the beautifully-mannered manager of the Sans Souci, who invited Luisa, myself and two other couples to dinner had no idea what he was letting himself in for. The appointed meeting place was the downstairs pool-side bar at 8 PM from where we would climb a flight of stairs to the restaurant. Between seven and eight a crowd of about twenty-two of our unit with their wives, all hotel guests and none of whom Andrew would wish to offend, had gathered in our corner. Nobody seemed to know who was on Andrew's list and who wasn't. Andrew was faced with a social dilemma; a quick conference with Derek Coyte and Dan Slater and Dan winkled out the chosen few from the crowd and whisked them off upstairs.The rest of the party took separate tables and we all got together again after dinner for dancing on the terrace. About an hour before turning-in time Jane Seymour, looking less tired than she should have done after a transatlantic trip, swept in from London with our costume designer, Julie Harris. They joined us just in time to hear Victor Davis of the *Daily Express*, embarking on one of his splendid stories none of which are repeatable. A great chap, Victor, with a fund of foreign travel tales to tell.

B-Day Thirty-two began with another high wind and a shift in schedule from the kite scene to the boats. Our Jamaican naval escort which steamed off mysteriously yesterday was back on our starboard side today after a drama of dimensions near to the cloak and dagger heart of Bond himself.

Included in the number of people who were privy to the information that the patrol boat was seconded to us, were, it seems, a group of ganja, or marijuana smugglers. They planned that while, quite literally, the coast was clear because the patrol boat was busy, a consignment would be shipped out. Equally aware of the opportunity were members of the US Federal Bureau of Investigation's narcotics squad who were involved because they knew the shipment was destined for the United States.

One report says the agents disguised themselves as part of

the film unit and complete with a camera waited offshore in a boat while the patrol boat lay in wait nearby. Whichever way the ambush was laid, it worked. The FBI boarded a yacht and found a colossal nine tons of ganja and arrested the crew. The ganja, which had been paid for in Jamaica, was taken ashore and burned.

The wind changed and as we had completed the day's sea shots, we went back to kiting. I dangled in the kite on the edge of the cliff-top, strung to the crane by what was said to be a thousand pound breaking point piece of wire. To me it looked exactly like the one hundred and twenty pound breaking point line we used for a fishing sequence a few days earlier that had snapped under a forty pound weight.

As I set off for one of my swings, 'Crackers', as David Cracknell has been dubbed, whispered that he didn't think the crane driver was all that bright upstairs. The driver was the man who had me as much at his mercy as an angler swinging a floundering fish on a line. By that time I had begun to feel less that bright upstairs myself. The combination of rum and bad shrimps the night before had given me a gyppy tummy, or what the British Army used to call the Cairo gallops. As I swung in the air, with the wind whipping the kite around, my stomach and I began to feel that the crew scattered fifty feet below might be in a very vulnerable position. When the call went to the crane driver to stop moving his giant jib the impetus carried me well over the cliff-edge with a clear view of the jagged rocks four hundred feet below. There was no back support or safety harness on the kite but I told myself that this was the stuff Bond pictures are made of and it should look good. Then a voice somewhere inside my head said: 'It will, if you live long enough to see it.'

Today, the last Thursday in November is Thanksgiving Day and Harry and Jackie threw a party at the Sans Souci for the unit. Harry engineered the whole thing and it was a magnificent production with a big buffet of turkeys, hams, tagliatelle, cranberry jelly, sweet potato and pumpkin pie and an endlessly flowing bar. The setting, overlooking the sea, was superb but I was puzzled that Harry who is a Canadian and Jackie who is Rumanian born with a French upbringing, should give an American-style Thanksgiving party for an English crew. Jackie was not very enlightening when I asked her why. She said simply: 'I like turkey.'

A calypso band imported from a local club kept up a cracking pace and delirious dancing went on into the small hours. At the party I renewed acquaintanceship with an old friend of mine, Boscoe Holder. He is here from his home in Trinidad visiting his New York-based brother, Geoffrey, who is playing Baron Samedi in *Live and Let Die*. Boscoe is the smaller brother, being only six feet three to Geoffrey's six feet six. We met when I was acting as stage manager at the Alexandra Palace in the good old days of British television when there were only two TV stages in the whole of the country. Boscoe brought the first limbo dancing and steel band to England and appeared in many of our musical shows with Benny Hill, who was our resident comedian, and the twelve-year-old Julie Andrews.

Boscoe and I had not seen each other for four years, when he appeared in a 'Saint' episode with me, so it was a happy reunion. When the band packed up, about twenty of us gathered round a grand piano on the open patio and to Boscoe's brilliant accompaniment we sang our way through a two hour repertoire ranging from 'Moonlight in Vermont' to a bouncing, 'Blame it on the Bossa Nova'. Luisa brought an entirely new flavour to calypsos by singing them in Italian.

Friday, B-Day Thirty-three. An underground location today in the vast Runaway Caves which are a magnificent Bondian setting. Seemingly endless miles of low ceiling and stalactites stabbing from the roof; the constant drip, drip of water which collects in underground lakes. Also there are bats; bats by the hundred. As Jane and I hared from one cave to another hounded by Mr Big's heavies, the bats fluttered around like so many autumn leaves and I told the General I thought it was very clever of him to arrange them. He said: 'Oh, yes. That's what is known as bat-ground action.'

We were lining up a shot in one of the caverns when Nick Hippisley-Coxe, clutching a bumper bundle of airmail appeared. It was just like mail time in the Army. 'Hello, Whitear, you've come in for a lot today.' George Whitear had five letters, all I got was bills.

Nick Hippisley-Coxe has brought an air of romance to the unit. In a few days his fiancée, Irish actress Sheelagh Cullen, arrives and they plan to marry here. There is no doubt that Nick is in for a lot of leg-pulling and practical joking before that happens. To make matters even livelier, it has been revealed that some years ago Nick took out our leading lady, Jane Seymour.

I have demanded a self-drive car. After due consideration, I would rather commit myself to the tender mercies of crazy crane drivers than to some of the local knights of the road. So for social occasions I will do the driving; but I will still be at the mercy of others for getting to and from the locations. I have no wish to come to a sticky end in a car unless I happen to be driving, and since the witch doctor told me I was in for a crash, I have become more nervous about motoring.

Coming back from location tonight I was only vaguely aware of the winding miles of road lined by acres of sugar cane, but I saw a cocky-looking little mongoose. They abound in Jamaica and some great, forward planner imported them in 1872 directly from India to kill off the cane field rats. Until then armies of boys had been employed to catch rats, and areas of cane growing land had to be given up because of their depredations. When they tired of their diet the mongoose turned on the snakes and thanks to their efforts Jamaica is snake-free, but they cannot have spent all their time hunting and eating because only nine, four males and five females, were imported a hundred years ago and now they number countless thousands. More recently they have acquired a taste for chicken and are creating a problem by depleting the local poultry population.

I got a note during dinner tonight from Ernie Smatt, a resident of the Island and friend of Linda Christian, who asked him to say hello. He came across to our table at the Sans Souci and invited us to his home for a drink. Ernie is a Jamaican of Lebanese origin with lucrative interests on the Island, and I do not think I have seen anything quite like his home in my life. Rows of Corinthian columns rolled away from each side of the front door which led into an indoor-outdoor open plan. There was a swimming pool shaped like a figure of eight. The bottom part of the eight was a dining area with a three foot channel of water running around a raised, carved teak dining suite. The various parts of the open plan were at different levels connected by small bridges and the whole place was surrounded by rocks and waterfalls. The South side of the house faced beaches and palms and, with the moon shining across the water, it looked magnificent. When *Dr No* was made in Jamaica, Ernie was approached to supply some of the boats for a substantial percentage of the film, but he says his prices apparently horrified the Production Company and he never heard again. He thought they were trying to hedge their bets and he did not pursue it, but bitterly regrets not doing so to this day.

Today is Saturday, packing day for the move to Montego Bay tomorrow for the last three weeks of the location. A friend of ours, John Bentley, the young millionaire whose company, Barclay Securities, recently took over British

Lion and Shepperton Studios, came to lunch. With him was actress, Viviane Ventura, and also at our table was Brenda Sweeney, who I had never met before although I know her uncle, Charles Sweeney, of the jet set and best backgammon circles.

My brother-in-law, Rudi, who is married to Luisa's sister, is landing in Kingston tonight from Rome. Unfortunately we won't be able to meet him because I am night shooting at Eden Falls where we shot my love scene with Gloria. Tonight's sequence is a night club scene where Baron Samedi and his sensuous voodoo dancers titillate the tourists with a mock obeah ceremony. In *Live and Let Die*, Baron Samedi's night club act is a cover for his real activities, because he is an obeah man in the pay of Mr Big.

Geoffrey Holder, besides being Baron Samedi, choreographed the dance sequences and auditioned dancers from Kingston. He rehearsed his golden-brown beauties on the terrace of the Sans Souci where their gyrations delighted hotel guests. As Baron Samedi, Geoffrey cuts a magnificent figure, his six feet six frame filling a white tail coat with a white top hat crowning his shaven head. A stark white mask of paint covers half his face, contrasting eerily with his own dark skin as he leads his lovelies in an obeah dance of death. Set against the splendour of cascading clouds of water, Baron Samedi like a towering tempest, swirls among the dancers, his long coat-tails flying while flaming torches light the scene and insistent drums tattoo relentless rhythm.

Tourist-filled tables ring the cabaret floor and as we spare no expense on a Bond film, the tourists are real! One of the assistants was sent round all the local hotels to ask guests if they would like to be in the night club scene. Those who agreed, obligingly donned evening dress, piled into the charabanc we sent for them and came down to the Ruin at Eden Falls to sit the night away on soft drinks while we shot the scene.

I am at this moment on stand-by, which is a terrible thing

on a Saturday night. I was sorely tempted to go out and get drunk, arrive on set and fall flat on my face. Like the professional I am, I resisted the temptation and will be on set stone cold sober at two o'clock in the morning.

Sunday morning, and 9 AM found us taking a last lingering look at the paradise of the Sans Souci before setting off on the sixty-seven-mile drive through palms and sugar plantations to Montego Bay where Luisa, the children and I have taken a villa on the legendary Rose Hall Estate. The Great House was the home of the infamous White Witch of Rose Hall, Annie Palmer, who in the middle of the nineteenth century ruled her sugar cane plantation with bestial cruelty and black magic. They say she was as beautiful as she was haughty, with a rich voice, black penetrating eyes and a deceptively soft mouth. She took great pleasure in personally flogging her terror-stricken slaves who believed implicitly in her power to conjure up such apparitions of doom as the three-legged horse and the rolling calf. She is said to have ridden her estates at night dressed as a man, laying her whip on the backs of slaves she found outdoors. She took many lovers among the white overseers of her plantation and treated them with utter contempt, demanding they be as merciless with the slaves as she was herself. She married and murdered three husbands by poison, stabbing and strangulation and was herself mysteriously strangled in her bedroom at Rose Hall in 1833 while still in her early thirties. Buried at Rose Hall Estate, her grave is marked by a blank stone.

The Great House fell into ruins after her death and three years ago it was restored to its original eighteenth century splendour at a cost of one million dollars by American businessman, John Rollins, who, fascinated by the land, the legend and the Great House, bought the Rose Hall plantation, with its thousands of acres and miles of beach-front.

It is a very romantic place to live, but I hope the stories of the White Witch walking the grounds at night are no more than local legend.

Our privately owned white-walled villa in the Rose Hall grounds overlooks Montego Bay. From a beautiful, blue swimming pool, surrounded by bougainvillaea, the lawns sweep down to the golf course. As we dined on the patio tonight a silent figure in blue loomed across the lawn carrying a single-barrelled twelve bore, which looked like a blunderbuss. He introduced himself as our personal security guard and adds a Bond-style touch to our staff of cook, maid and butler.

Monday morning and a rest day. I saw virtually no one from the unit all day. Unlike Ocho Rios where we stayed in two hotels, the unit here is stretched out in hotels all the way along the coast. Guy and Kerima have a villa half a mile from us, Harry and Jackie's villa is a mile away and Derek Coyte and Dan Slater are just down the hill, very pleased with the villa they are renting from the man who invented the jet engine, Sir Frank Whittle.

Jane Seymour, who spent the day with us, is bewailing her fate in a hotel on the beach which caters for American tourists in the worst possible way. Everyone is expected to sit down to dinner at the same time at long trestle tables and between courses donkey races and egg and spoon races take place.

This morning we took an eight mile trip down to Montego Bay to one of the biggest supermarkets I have ever seen. They sell everything from pins to elephants. I must have bought most things in between because it was not one of my lighter shopping bills – 250·00 Jamaican dollars (£125) and that's a lot of papaya.

Ernie Smatt invited John Bentley, Viviane Ventura and Jane Seymour along with Luisa and myself to spend the rest of the day on his forty-five foot Hatteras power-boat. We cruised around Montego Bay, dodging the water skiers and once a jumbo jet, which swept so low in front of us to land at the sea front airport, that we had to reverse engines or it would have taken the top off our superstructure. It was absolutely beautiful to rock gently on the calm, blue bay, the contrasting coral below, and watch those beautiful jet birds swoop from the sky puffing white smoke from their wheels as they touch down.

We lunched on hamburgers at a Montego Bay restaurant then headed out to deep water for some fishing. We cast six lines in rather choppy water and as the bows went down into the waves we suddenly saw three dolphins right in front of us. Our boat followed them and they were obviously playing a game. Their cavorting frightened the fish away so I took my Super Eight up on the bridge to shoot some cine film.

My view from the bridge was of the lovely Viviane Ventura, who had taken off her bikini top. She looked like the ship's figure-head. Luisa was taking pictures of Jane in the stern and knew I was shooting on the bridge but I don't think she knew what!

'Ganja Joe Died from Smoking – Aged 12' read the inscription on the gravestone. An eerie epitaph for one so young. Other stones chronicled similar strange and sudden deaths. The letters ALLELUJAH carved over a nearby church seemed to foretell not salvation, but doom.

This was the meticulously detailed set the Art Department created for the cemetery scene where Baron Samedi from behind a gravestone fills the air with the strains of a foreboding flute. When he hits top C an antenna shoots up, then twisting it in two he reveals a microphone through which he reports to Mr Big on Bond's movements.

The scene was set on a chalky hill three miles off the main

Montego Bay to Falmouth road. I arrived at 7 AM to begin B-Day Thirty-four and found my caravan had been propped up on the sloping hill-side by some Heath Robinson method of blocks and stones. Inside, the floor sloped at an angle of forty-five degrees and Jane Seymour clung gamely to a chair while Paul, balancing on long tanned legs which disappear into carefully frayed denim shorts, aimed a sponge with unerring accuracy at her lovely face. The term 'my caravan' is a loose one; it is used for everything from make-up to hairdressing, changing room for all and sundry not to mention my invaluable green bucket.

The day was heavy and overcast and before long the rain teemed down and turned the hill-side into a chalky torrent. It rains hard but not for long in a Jamaican December and the sun soon peeked through. 'Crackers' called me out of my caravan for a rehearsal; I took two steps and sprawled on my backside in a most unsecret agent-like mess of mud and chalk. Luckily, I had not changed into my Bond outfit. The soggy chalk permeated to my skin and I am glad no stray tourist peeked into our mock church to see me changing my underpants on one side of the altar while Solitaire slipped out of her bra on the other.

We wrapped shooting at 4.30 PM and I was bounced the three miles back by my 'exclusive' driver screaming that his exclusivity had been violated. He had been sent to pick up some field workers who had been helping prepare the cemetery site and he was very uptight about it.

'Me!' he yelled, 'who has driven Jamaican Prime Ministers, visiting Prime Ministers and Lord Beaverbrook in my car; having to drive field workers! Never again!'

B-Day Thirty-five, and our location was a derelict wharf surrounded by burnt-out warehouses in the heart of Montego Bay. The only building still standing was the fire station. I suppose the brigade were on their tea break when the fire broke out. The sequence was where Bond and Rosie Carver arrive at the wharf in a Mini-Moke to board Quarrel's boat.

It must have been the hottest day so far and I had to get in and out of the Mini-Moke, each time heaving a heavy hamper from the back. By the time we got to the fifth take the sweat was pouring off me and I was beginning to wish Glorious Gloria would get it right. Afterwards she confessed to me that her mind was not on her work because she had just seen her mother off on the plane home to New York and she was missing her. I told her the way she was working this morning she should have put herself on the plane and left her mother to play the scene, which made her laugh and cheered her up.

We finally got it in the can and I returned to the comparative cool of my caravan to be interviewed by a local radio reporter. He had been among those journalists who, on my arrival in Jamaica, had been obsessed with my fee for Bond. He set his tape recorder in motion and dived straight in on the same tack.

'The entire show business world is buzzing with what you are getting,' said he.

'It's not buzzing at all,' said I, refusing to be drawn.

He then asked me if I had been a professional actor for a number of years, and I assured him a number of critics didn't think so; at the same time feeling it necessary to point out that the only difference between an amateur actor and a professional was that the latter got paid.

'Mr Lew Grade—' he began.

I interrupted to say that he could call me Roger or anything else but had to call Lew 'Sir'. I could tell by his expression he thought I was putting him on. He then asked me the most lunatic leading question of the year which was:

'Is your Bond going to be *better* than Sean Connery's Bond?'

When he had finished he wanted to play the whole thing

back so he could erase and alter, not my answers, but his questions. At this point I was rescued by a call to work.

He wasn't the only one with a hang-up today. Chris Doll, our Television Producer, approached me halfway through the morning, when I was sitting there wringing with sweat, to give up my lunch hour and do a shot for his television special. He had set up a camera at the Governor's house and Geoffrey Holder was to tell a voodoo story while Jane, Gloria and I sat round and listened.

As lunchtime neared it became apparent that the wharf sequence would soon be in the can and we could return to the chalky hill in the afternoon for a couple more takes on the graveyard sequence. The lunch break came and thrusting some cold lamb down my throat and grabbing an ice-cream, I leapt into a car to go up to the Governor's residence all ready to listen to Geoffrey's voodoo story, but there was no Geoffrey, and no Jane either. An assistant had pinched their car, but in any case they had been side-tracked and sent for make-up ready for our return to the graveyard. Chris Doll was in such a state of agitation I couldn't even take the mickey out of him.

I moved off to the graveyard but to get there I passed our villa and stopped for a quick dip in the pool with my children, much to their delight. They are beginning to doubt they have a father lately, they see so little of me.

Bond Day Thirty-six; or better C for Crocodile Day. After weeks of waiting we meet at last. The location was a crocodile safari farm about twenty miles from our villa run by Ross Kananga, an American who is part Seminole Indian. Ross has lent his surname to *Live and Let Die*. Tom Mankiewicz, the scriptwriter, liked the sound of the name Kananga and has called one of our characters Dr Kananga after him.

He has over 1,300 crocodiles and alligators and the unique

ability to coax them to him by imitating their mating calls. Ross , whose father, a crocodile wrestler, was killed by them, has spent his life with them and has the scars to prove it, but he still holds them in some bewildering form of affection. When the General was at the farm for a recce weeks before he began shooting, he asked Ross how he could tell the difference between the males and the females and Ross said: 'Oh, that's easy. The girls have such pretty, petite faces.'

This morning I was bleary-eyed at the early start but I soon woke up when we passed a sign which said 'Beware Crocodiles Crossing', then stopped at another which warned: 'Trespassers Will be Eaten'. That was not bluff, as somewhere among the log-like mass in the swamp is Bongus, a 13-foot-long, 1,500-pounder who once ate four fishermen.

The atmosphere was tense and Guy had refused admission to visitors or even our photographers. The unit was cut to the minimum number essential to shoot the scene. Joining us for the first time in this far from jolly situation today was Julius Harris, a beaming black mountain of a man who plays Tee Hee, the chilling heavy who has a steel snipping claw on his artificial arm. Today's scene is where Bond is in captivity and ominously introduced to the crocodiles by Tee Hee, who is casually feeding them chicken with his claw.

Crocs apparently can go for many months without food and these had not been fed for fourteen weeks to keep them lively, because a well-fed croc is a quiet, sleepy croc. I noticed that they seemed very glad to see us and hoped they understood that it was chicken on the menu, not actor.

The morning was overcast, the legacy of heavy overnight rain which made the mosquitoes in the crocodile swamp as lively as the crocs. We sprayed ourselves with a Jamaican insecticide called 'Off' which is far too polite a trade name to intimidate mosquitoes. It should be 'B-Off' or 'F-Off'.

The key to cooperation from the crocs is Ross Kananga's crocodile call. He puts his fingers beneath his chin and then after a lot of heaving in the lower regions of his body a sound streams from his throat which is a cacophonous cross between the mating of a sex-starved snail and that of a pig being raped by an elephant. With this, large lumps of seemingly inanimate muddy log slide down the banks and through the water towards Kananga.

Julius and I watched, sweating and waiting on jelly knees, and whatever kind of call Ross made they sure as hell came. Julius was handicapped by his arm which is a very intriguing contrivance. It is strapped to him round his chest and the opening and closing of the claw is controlled by his breathing. He has not had time to master the use of it. He had wanted it to be sent to New York so that he could practice with it, but it had to be shipped straight from London to Jamaica because the wardrobe department needed it here to measure it and cut his suits so that they would fit when he was wearing it.

As the crocs slithered around, Julius struggled manfully to claw up the chicken and fling it at their snapping jaws. One piece stuck to his claw and a croc seemed to have its eye on it so Julius backed up somewhat smartly; then another piece of chicken fell to his feet unnoticed by us, but not by an eight foot croc which was torpedoeing towards us to get it, until someone kicked the grisly lump of chicken into the swamp and the croc snapped it.

Crocs are the most malevolent, menacing creatures I have come across. They can move at forty miles per hour on land, leap their own length by springing themselves with their tail and are so fast they can catch a low-flying bird. Ross Kananga's largest croc stretches some twenty feet long and over sixty years old. What sort of a mess that would make I shudder to think, when even a three-footer can mangle a man's hand.

They do not like to be disturbed, but are fearless to the

point of arrogance when they feel like it. Nothing seems to stand in their way except alligators and we have quite a few of those in the mangrove swamps. Although alligators are not so prone to polishing off human beings, they can play havoc with the crocodiles. One broke into a pen holding five crocs killed two and injured three, which shouldn't happen to anything except crocodiles.

During lunch Chris Doll asked if I would sit with Gloria and Jane and listen to Geoffrey Holder telling the voodoo story he had tried to film a few days earlier. I stuffed a few forkfuls of hasty food down my throat and shot off in the car. After waiting for a precious fifteen minutes while Gloria, who was not working today, changed her dress, I lost my ex-Saint-like smile and sent someone to tell Gloria that there are three other stars in the film who were working this afternoon, and to get herself moving.

Geoffrey began his yarn about some eight-year-old boy falling in the dust and how his mother stuck a candle in his mouth. It was such a let-down I felt like sticking a candle into Geoffrey somewhere else.

After lunch we were back with the crocs. Ross Kananga was concerned because the crew were being a bit free and easy with the crocodiles and he feared an accident. Some of the unit were turning their backs on them when they were only a few feet away and that is not the wisest thing to do. Crocs glide a few feet nearer when you are not looking, then stop motionless in water without causing a ripple hoping you will not notice. Ross repeatedly warned the unit and said it would take an accident to teach them. I hope not.

When a crocodile strikes it will go for a limb, a leg or arm and strip the bone of all flesh before locking its teeth on the broadest part of the bone. Then it throws itself backwards in the water, spinning with its incredibly strong tail until it detaches the limb from the body.

Harry came out to the crocodile farm mid-afternoon and said that tomorrow the main unit would switch back to the

Roger and Luisa on location

Deborah and Geoffrey arrive from London

Speedboat chase

Funeral with a difference

Roger Moore teaching leading lady Jane Seymour all about guns

A tense moment in the terrifying voodoo sequence

Rehearsing for the grotto fight

There are two ways of getting black eyes . . .

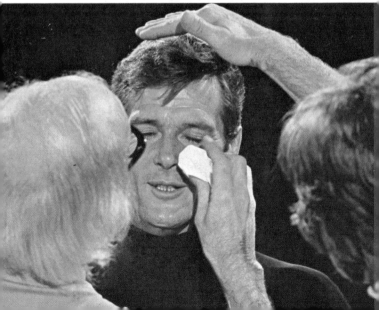

Flying high in the kite sequence

Gloria Hendry, who plays Rosie, is greeted by Roger Moore and daughter, Deborah

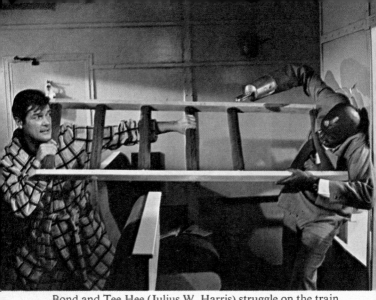

Bond and Tee Hee (Julius W. Harris) struggle on the train

Bond and Mr Big battle underwater in the grotto

bus sequence, while the second unit stayed to get some painstaking shots of the crocs crunching their chicken.

This evening Luisa and I had an excellent dinner of American prime rib at the Rose Hall Golf Club down the bougainvillaea and hibiscus-fringed lane which winds from the front of our villa. After dinner we watched part of a movie projected on to an outdoor screen. Under the inky sky with twinkling stars in the flower-filled club grounds, it was very romantic.

B-Day Thirty-seven began with a phone call from George Whitear, the unit photographer, complaining bitterly that his driver had overslept and he had no way of getting to the location. I drove to his hotel to pick him up and we set out on what we were promised was a two and a half hour drive. It turned out to be a three hour nightmare with one of the hairiest drivers I have ever met in my life. He drove in typical Jamaican fashion, all over the road at what seems to be the regulation speed of ninety miles an hour.

If the drive was bad, Alligator Pond, our location for the day, was worse. When the world needs an enema, Alligator Pond is where they will stick the nozzle. The area is scarred with bauxite quarries where the red alumina clay is dug up and ferried out on huge trucks that churn the roads to mud ruts in the rain and dry dust bowls in the hot sun. The centre of the village is a T-junction; a little hump of dirt dropping straight down into a bay where this morning the fishermen were dragging in their nets. The dusty street was full of pigs, chickens and dogs; children ran about starkers. The villagers milled around us open-mouthed, wondering what the hell had happened to their sleepy little village. I don't think they had even seen a motion picture before, let alone one in the making.

There wasn't much motion picture-making going on with *Live and Let Die* when we arrived. George Crawford, the location caterer, had borrowed one of the cars first thing this morning and gone off in search of biscuits. The car he borrowed happened to be the one with the make-up in it, so Jane sat for two hours in my trailer waiting for him to come back before she could be prepared for the fray of the day. George arrived back shortly after and faced a very fed-up Guy Hamilton.

The scene we were shooting is where Solitaire and 007, having discovered Dr Kananga's illicit poppy fields, are making their escape. They reach the village and clash with police, in cars and on motor bikes. Their only escape vehicle is a double-decker bus which Bond spies parked outside a café.

It was to be a day of disasters; my trailer was parked on the street and as I sat inside waiting to be called on set, there was a terrifying crunch which rocked the trailer and sent me sprawling. A six ton lorry had crashed straight into the side of my caravan. There is now a gaping hole where my green bucket used to be; thank God nobody was sitting on it at the time.

Bernard Hanson, the location manager, turned up in the afternoon with the good news that instead of a long draggy ride home by car we would be going by plane. He said there would be two seats at 4.30 PM and three at 5.30 PM.

So, at 4.10 PM, having finished the last shot, I was shipped into a car with Jane Seymour and driven to a tiny 200 yard concrete airstrip to catch the 4.30 PM plane. We arrived to find the plane sailing overhead and we were faced with an hour's wait in the heat under a wooden roof in the company of a flea-ridden dog with a blind eye and three Jamaican kids bopping away to the local DJ Radio Show.

After a while Guy, Derek Cracknell and Ted Moore joined us, the hour passed and the 5.30 PM plane for Montego Bay took off with the five of us aboard. Jane plumped for the front seat next to the pilot and her first flying lesson, which was not conducive to a steady stomach for the rest of us. Nervous glances flew like a mad mosquito between the General, 'Crackers', Ted and myself when Jane took over the controls. Coincidentally, we were flying over cockpit country and the four of us fancied staying in our cockpit to a crash landing in that wild and weird land. It is the home of the Maroons, who are the descendants of slaves who ran away when the British fought Spain for possession of the island. It took five years for the English to drive the Spanish out and during that time the slaves who fled to the mountains proclaimed their independence. For the next eighty years, from 1661, the British tried to subdue them without success. Finally, they negotiated a treaty and signed it not only in ink, but blood, which was drawn from both the English and the Maroons. They mixed the blood with rum and drank it, then intoxicated with their own bloody diplomacy both sides slid into a state of strange truce which still exists.

The people of this state within a state, are proud. They make their own laws and are exempt from Jamaican taxes. The roads are impassable and the only way to get into Maroon country is by sending a telegram and saying what time your car will be arriving at a given point on the road, and if permission to visit is granted, you are met and escorted in on a donkey. There is conflict in their ranks now about whether they should allow themselves to become the tourist attraction they have for so long resisted.

From the air the country looks like a series of vast cockpits with little shacks set amongst Palms. Ted Moore, who is single-minded where his hobby is concerned, thought it looked like a gigantic golf course and Guy, spotting a few rivers, was ruminating on the possibility of staging another motor boat chase there. In no time at all we were over the twinkling lights of Montego Bay; a smooth touch down and home in time for tea.

*　　*　　*

Today we were working on the lovely road to Lucea for B-Day Thirty-eight. It runs from Montego Bay through sugar cane, high wooded hills and then drops to skirt the palms and sea. Somewhere along the road I am literally going to catch a bus. At this stage in the plot Bond becomes a bus driver, I jump into the driving seat, Jane clambers aboard and we use it to escape from pursuing police.

This bus, which was shipped over from London, is a normal double decker which has spent the best years of its life on the London no 19 run. It has been resprayed from its London Transport red to a muddy mixture of greys and greens which the Art Department decided would be the colours of the fictitious San Monique transport.

Everyone who has ever travelled on a double-decker will have had the dizzy, dreadful thought of what would happen if the bus drove under a low bridge. During the bus chase sequence we are going to find out and the bus has been specially prepared for it. The upper deck has been cut away and placed on rollers so that when the crash comes it will shoot spectacularly backwards leaving Bond and Solitaire in the bottom half to escape under the bridge; the top and bottom decks are temporarily bolted together for the chase build-up to the crash. All this is much more easily said than done; the sequence will take several days to shoot.

In charge of the bus and here to teach me how to handle it is Maurice Patchett, a London Transport Bus Driving Instructor, who has flown in for what must be one of the oddest jobs any driving instructor has been paid to do: to teach somebody how to drive a bus and successfully smash it.

We arrived and there was the double-decker looking quite incongruous, parked among the palms a few yards from the lapping Caribbean. George Crawford's catering tables were lined neatly by the sea-side and I sat down for a quick cup of coffee, when I learned of another disaster the day before. The forty-seater coach, which carries the crew to and from their hotels, had been hit on a hill by my trailer going backwards. Apparently, the trailer driver had stopped, not put his handbrake on and it rolled back, crashing into the coach. No one was hurt but it smashed the coach windscreen and the crew had a very breezy drive back.

Today was to be less spectacular, but brightened by a visit from Luisa, who took some photographs for this book, and my son Geoffrey.

This afternoon George Whitear, our photographer, appeared with a look of blank amazement on his face, muttering something about a coconut and pointing at his camera. While he was standing under a tree a falling coconut had hit his camera and smashed the shutter. Such are the trials of the tropics.

B-Day Thirty-nine was a slow day. The weather was heavy and overcast all morning, but by lunchtime the sun was out and burning down on us with its usual vigour. We were on the road to Lucea again for more of the bus chase, mainly bits, pieces and preparation. The road on which we filmed part of the chase is used by normal traffic and our assistants were kept very busy holding up cars while we shot. One gentleman, in a smart Mercedes Benz, took less than kindly to being stopped and the exasperated assistant finally shouted:

'You can't drive through here, Sir.'

'I think I can, young man,' came the crushing retort. 'It's my land you are standing on.'

I had an insatiable desire all morning for a piece of chocolate, which is not on 007's diet, and in any case we were fifteen miles from the nearest shop.

Some years ago while shooting an episode of 'The Saint' at a theatre in Watford, I bought about a fiver's worth of chocolate and shared it out amongst the crew, very sweet of me, if you'll pardon the pun. In amongst the candy I slipped an unwrapped bar of Ex Lax and presented it to Tony Wager, one of the cast. I watched him eat the whole bar, then I sent someone to the nearest chemist for a couple of rolls of toilet paper, a plastic bucket and a bottle of anti-dysentery mixture. I got the painter to inscribe the bucket with Tony's name and made the presentation: not a very nice thing to do. He felt no ill effects until that evening when his wife had prepared a dinner party for him. A couple of years later, he had his revenge when Luisa and I drove up to Luton to see Shirley Bassey at Caesar's Palace and discovered that Tony Wager was the compère. Spying me in the audience, he bathed me in a spotlight, got me on my feet and proceeded to tell the audience the whole story. My face was redder than his rear end had been a couple of years earlier.

From past episodes to the future; the mail today brought a couple of scripts from Producer, Elliott Kastner. *Sleep is for the Rich,* is one and the other a proposed series of Westerns along the lines of a cowboy Bond called 'Morgan Kane'. My American Agent called to discuss a film for MGM with Charlton Heston, but the script won't be ready for a couple of weeks. George Barrie telephoned too, this morning. He is President of Fabergé, the company I joined in an executive capacity a couple of years ago, along with Cary Grant. George is planning on winging in this week-end in one of our company jets, which has to be seen to be believed. It seats fifteen in very fine style. The centre of the cabin is monopolized by a mammoth electric organ, installed for George, who cheerfully challenges the heavenly harpists as he cloud hops across the Atlantic.

It's a pity the plane isn't large enough to take the unit back to London. Harry tells me we are having problems getting a charter flight out of here on the 20 December, because the flight BOAC had arranged was pre-empted by a Canadian group and it looks as though we might all be stuck here for Christmas. I would not be too disturbed by the thought, but

102

there would be a revolt amongst the crew who would miss their wives, children and Christmas cheer.

Guess who's coming to dinner? Sidney Poitier, who else? He lives in Nassau and is hoping to hop over next week to spend a couple of days with us. Michael Caine was coming from London, but he has been laid low with the 'flu and doesn't feel up to the transatlantic flight. Mike is not the only 'flu victim. Roddy Mann, *Sunday Express* columnist and an old chum from way back, whom I was looking forward to chatting to, is ill and has had to cancel his visit.

While the first unit has been busy filming the voodoo cemetery, the wharf scene and chasing buses, the second unit has been in amongst the swamps of the crocodile farm. Yesterday they were involved in a typical Kananga-like clash, when one crocodile came out of the water and was making determinedly for the camera crew. Kananga tackled it with a grappling hook and ropes, but when its mouth and feet were tied its lashing tail broke his little-toe. He carried on until he had slung the crocodile back into the water and only then attended to his toe, which was sticking out at right angles from his foot. He said simply he did not want the crocodiles going around eating any of the unit because it would be bad publicity.

If I never get another film role after *Live and Let Die*, I can always get a job on the buses. To qualify as a London bus driver takes ten days' instruction and Maurice says I am doing quite nicely. The cab of a London bus is full of gadgets, like the little hook above your left ear which is the starter. To select a gear, you hit another button which picks up the gear; nothing like the normal gear shift. Maurice was particularly careful to explain the function of a little red flag that drops down in an emergency.

'When you see that,' he warned, 'put your foot down on

the brake and don't lift it off again because you don't get a second chance. It means your brakes have gone.'

We were filming the sequence where Bond and Solitaire take the bus and drive off with the police in hot pursuit. I am in the cab and Solitaire is in the back. For the first shot I had to drive the bus fast for twenty feet where an electrician stood with sun reflector boards to get the proper lighting effect. The boards were striking the sun right into my eyes and as I took off as fast as I could, it was difficult to see where to stop. I did it four times, each time getting a little faster and more dashing, so the sparks with the reflector boards was side-stepping more rapidly each time. On the last take I hit the brake and down came the red flag; I kept my foot down hard and pulled on the hand brake. If Maurice hadn't told me about it there would have been one electrician as flat as his reflector board, under a fifty-five ton London bus.

Our Baby Jane is brave as well as beautiful. She literally puts her life in my hands when she boards our bouncing bus, and to keep her smiling I threaten to get her a Clippie's uniform and ticket punch.

This morning I noticed plaster on Maurice's wrist and asked him what had happened. He told me that the road I would drive on today, which is full of pot-holes anyway, had been strewn with boulders and thick branches by the Property Department to give a better bumpy effect. Maurice had taken the bus for a trial run down the road, jolted over a bad bump and the wheel whipped round injuring his wrist. I held on to the wheel like grim death when it was my turn and it really does spin round. I am not allowed a seat belt and I must have hit my head on the roof ten times.

Apart from the gadgets in the bus cab, there is a walkie-talkie clamped above my head connected to 'Crackers' and to the posse of 'police' on motor bikes. The radio reception is terrible, and all I could make out was Derek saying:

'Right. On "Action" just take off.'

. Then I heard something like:

'Turn right and keep going down the road and keep going fast, the police are after you.'

So, I took off, Jane bouncing around in the back, not quite sure how far I was supposed to go. I swung out on to the narrow main road, heaved the bus round the bend and drove for five miles without finding anywhere to turn round and go back for another shot. The road was hung with low trees and the bus top, which has yet to be smashed off, was clipping the branches and knocking them all over the bloody place. Eventually I found what looked like a turning where I could reverse the bus, which is a four-handed job at the best of times. I started reversing and the bus shuddered to a stop. I looked back out of the cab and there was a thick branch sticking through the back window. I had to get out, dislodge it and drive further up the road to find another place to turn. On one side, the road fell away to the sea and on the other side the drive of someone's house sloped sharply up hill. The bus resisted the hill and it took countless manoeuvres, and a lot of sweat to turn round while a queue of cars formed along the road. Finally, I made it and drove back up the road to find Guy and Ted Moore sitting in the car smiling and all ready to go home. The take had been perfect and my exertions to turn the wretched thing round for another take, had been a waste of time. What an end to B-Day Forty!

B-Day Forty-one and on with the bus chase. In this scene three stunt drivers, dressed as motor cycle patrol policemen, on huge Harley Davidsons, bat down the curving hill between sugar cane fields after Bond's bus. At the bottom, where a pump has spewed out water over a six hundred foot square road area, Bond's double-decker brakes and slews round in a tight, wet 180 degrees arc and heads back up the hill scattering two police cars chasing him. One car careers down a bank, the other scythes two hundred yards through eight foot high sugar cane flanking the road. The motor cyclists can't stop; one flies sixty feet over the sea wall on to a coral reef, the second smacks in to the bus side and the third hurtles off the road. The scene will take up sixty seconds worth of screen time at the local cinema and three long days to shoot in the blazing sun.

At the top of the hill the unit spread out along the roadside like an army in retreat. There was George Crawford's mobile kitchen which, when cooking is in progress, tags another ten degrees on the existing ninety degree temperature. George and Tony, his cook, with their white clad assistants, sweat their way through the pots and pans preparing the miracle of the loaves and fishes, in the shape of lamb chops, steaks or the great local delicacy, curried goat. I stick to cheese, cold meat and mustard pickle. Twenty tables and a hundred chairs fill up the space between prop van, camera car, sound car, generators, electrical vans and thirty-odd other vehicles from police car chevrolets to the unit bus. A bloody great mess of a camp site which attracts an unending straggle of sightseers, straining their necks to watch our sweating struggle against time.

In spite of all this murder and mayhem on the mountain, romance is still in the air and Nick's wedding will definitely take place on Saturday. It was to have been a rest day, but Harry says that if we are going to be home for Christmas we have to work. This was decided last night at a meeting in the Production Office, and someone asked about Nick's wedding. At that moment Nick was passing the door.

Harry said: 'Young man.'

'Yes Sir.'

'What time is the wedding?'

'Four o'clock.'

'We are going to work until four, you can get married at 5.30.'

'Thank you, Sir.'

So it is on, and we are busy thinking up wording for the mock call sheet we are having printed.

Jane will be Matron of Honour and I have agreed to be Best Man.

Today was tear off the bus top day. I arrived in the main street of Lucea for B-Day Forty-two to find soggy breakfast tables and George Crawford almost in tears trying to serve breakfast as the rain for the third time that morning turned his fried eggs to poached.

A long avenue lined with huts and palm fronds led to a bridge flanked by two small hills where the top of the bus was to be knocked off. Controlling the crowds of sightseers was an impossible task. Just as we thought we had cleared the roadside for the shot and the cameras began to turn a black face would peep out of the palms, the General would shout 'Cut' and back we would go to start again. Eventually we got most of the rubber necks up on the hill out of camera range, but it was a bit like the cowboy movie when someone says: 'There's not an Indian within a hundred miles of here' as an arrow goes through his chest.

Controlling the crowd when filming in a public place is never easy. Once when shooting a 'Saint' episode at the Tower of London a gent with a couple of days' growth and a copy of *Sporting Life* under his arm, who was right in the way of our shot, refused to join the rest of the sightseers herded out of camera range. Nobody knew quite what to do when Ian Hendry, who was playing a police inspector, had a flash of inspiration .

He approached the man quietly from behind and said:
'Haven't seen you in this manor before, have I, Charlie?'
'No, Inspector,' said the man, nervously edging away. 'I am terribly sorry, I am clean and I won't do it again. I am sorry.' He touched his forelock and fled into the crowd.

On another 'Saint' episode which I was directing at

107

Waterloo Station, we had set up a shot with a great deal of care where I was to walk down some steps towards the cameras. Just as I started off with cameras rolling a little fellow dashed up towards me and said:

'I know you! You're Patrick McGoohan. Gawd luv ya, come and 'ave a drink.'

He was grabbed and hustled off and we began again. I was supposed to be in disguise for the scene and wore a pair of horn rimmed glasses and an old duffle coat. I started down the steps and a voice floated clearly from the watching crowd:

'Cor! That Roger Moore don't look half as smart as 'e do on the telly.'

We got the road clear at last and the camera covered all angles of the bus belting down to the bridge before we got to the actual shot where it goes under the bridge and the top slices off. Not only had we carefully cut the upper deck of the bus for a clean separation during the smash but we had also built the bridge.

As the bus engine revved for the final run, tension among the unit and the collected crowd of about four hundred tautened. 'Crackers' ' call of 'Roll 'em', putting the cameras in motion, preceded Guy's cry for 'Action' and the bus began its boulder-strewn run for the bridge. Movie cameras covered from three angles and countless stills cameras clicked as the bus smashed the bridge spot on the front destination sign and the top crunched backwards as if sliced from some giant egg.

The bottom half, carrying Jane, belted under the bridge and there were seconds of silence, as the sound recorders were still running, before everyone burst into a cheer. Nobody knew exactly what would happen when the top came off and I admired little Jane Seymour's guts as she sat in the speeding bus heading for the bridge and the big bang. I have a feeling her eyes were tight shut.

The crash came before lunch and there was a carnival

atmosphere, a mingling of relief and celebration during the meal. The festival air had flattened by the time our dessert courses came at the sight of scores of young, hungry black faces flanking both sides of the road where the lunch tables were laid. George Crawford fed dozens from food that was left and when we moved back to the cameras they pinched everything that was moveable from salt and pepper pots, sauce bottles, bread, biscuits, not to mention four tables.

B-Day Forty-three. B for Best Man Day. Nick and Sheelagh stood barefoot on the sand under an arch of tropical flowers to be joined in holy matrimony by a black Episcopalian minister in a surf-side ceremony; the wackiest, wildest wedding the island has ever seen.

The mock call sheet said 'fivish'; the place, the beach of the Colony Hotel where most of the unit are staying. Luisa and I, with Deborah and Geoffrey, arrived on the beach to find the caressing Caribbean breeze had become an excited whirl and flying sand hit us like red hot needles. The assembled unit, standing stoically in the wind, were scattered by a sudden, swift downpour which sent us all scurrying for shelter under the coconut leaf roof of the beach bar where champagne glasses were lined up ready to toast the bridal pair. Luckily the bride was late or we would have been halfway through the ceremony when the rain came. She sat in a car outside the hotel waiting for the 'Father of the Bride', Derek Cracknell, whose car, we later learned, had broken down on the way from location. The part was hastily recast and the bride came down the beach on the arm of Derek Coyte, with Jane Seymour as Matron of Honour in attendance.

What to wear to a beach wedding requires some thought on the part of the bride. Sheelagh looked lovely in a diaphanous lilac top with a bare midriff and matching skirt which swept the sand. It was so windy she had to keep one hand on her large brimmed hat and with the other hand in Nick's, offered a splendid view of bra-less cleavage to the officiating minister, the Reverend Percy Thompson. I don't know how he managed to keep his mind on the marriage vows.

He began by asking Nick what he was and Nick looked blank.

'Pardon?' he said politely.

The minister repeated the question, at the same time tapping the black bound Bible in his hand. The penny dropped and Nick said vaguely, 'I suppose you could call me C of E.'

'What's that?' asked the minister.

'Episcopalian,' I interjected hastily, to head off a sectarian squabble. The Reverend Percy thumbed his way through the book to find the appropriate service and Nick asked anxiously:

'It's not too long, is it?'

I perpetually nudged him in the arm and told him it was not too late to change his mind. It's a pity Derek Cracknell got held up because when they got to that bit about does anybody know why these two should not be joined together we were going to say Nick had a wife and six kids in England.

The audience, sorry congregation, was gathered a few feet away and the wind was so loud they could not hear one word of the service. They realized it was over when the minister said 'You can kiss the bride,' and I kissed Nick.

Chris Doll, hopping like some large blond sandfly, directed his television crew, as they committed the scene to celluloid posterity. Cameras clicked throughout the service, including those of a couple of tourists who strayed down the beach to see what was going on and stayed to take pictures. Above the voice of the Reverend Percy intoning the marriage service Harry could plainly be heard telling them to get the hell off the beach as this was a private wedding.

Sheelagh hitched her pretty voile skirt and we struggled through stinging sand and autograph hunters to the reception. Guests gathered in Coco's Beach Bar for champagne and wedding cake and a calypso band played a Caribbean version of the wedding march. The wind dropped, the moon shone, champagne flowed, the dancers spilled from the bar on to the sand and the whole affair turned into what is known in the best circles as a right do.

With us at the wedding was the widely syndicated American columnist, Rex Reed, who moviegoers will remember played a part in *Myra Breckenridge*. I had invited Rex to dinner but I had forgotten my cash and had to borrow from Derek Coyte and Dan Slater to cover the bill. Bond would never be so forgetful!

Today's location, B-Day Forty-four, was up a five mile muddy track to the spot where, in the film, Jimmy Bond and Solitaire discover Dr Kananga's camouflaged crop of drug producing poppies.

After a seven-mile drive through drizzle on the surfaced road from the villa, Wilfred, my Jamaican driver, slithered rather than drove up the bumpy, boggy approach. The weather was windy as well as wet and when we arrived unit members were picking their way gingerly over the chalky treacherous surface where a slip could mean at best a wet backside and at worst an injured back.

George Crawford's mobile kitchen was poised on a bend about fifty yards from where Wilfred parked so I joined the company of slitherers and edged my way up to persuade Tony the cook to make a couple of egg and bacon sandwiches for Jane, who had just arrived, and myself. The caravan had not yet negotiated the track so Jane and I munched the sandwiches in the shelter of my car.

The weather forecast had been for heavy showers and cloud, but the General and 'Crackers' were optimistically

EON PRODUCTIONS LIMITED

CALL SHEET

No: 21A(JAMAICA)

TIME ARRIVE SET: 5.00.'ish.

EXT. THE WEDDING AND RECEPTION

Scene 1 - THE COLONY HOTEL BEACH   DAY/DUSK

ARTISTE	CHARACTER	ON SET
MISS SHEELAGH CULLEN	THE BRIDE	5.00.pm 'ish.
MR. NICHOLAS HIPPISLEY-COXE	THE GROOM	5.00.pm 'ish.
MR. DEREK CRACKNELL	BRIDE'S FATHER	5.00.pm 'ish.
MR. ROGER MOORE	BEST MAN	5.00.pm 'ish.
PERCY THOMPSON	MARRIAGE OFFICER	5.00.pm 'ish.

STAND-INS: NOT REQUIRED. THANK YOU VERY MUCH.

EXTRAS:

6 MEN   WAITERS   S/BY TILL CALLED
THE UNIT   WEDDING GUESTS   5.00.pm 'ish.

PROPS: The ring. Champagne.

CATERING: Reception buffet and drinks.

TRANSPORT: Coach to take unit straight to Colony Hotel on completion of shooting and stand-by for return. Unit cars -- as above.

WARDROBE: Due to the lack of response to the Moss Bros fitting, dress should be very casual.

MAKE-UP: Tears (croc. type).

HAIR: Should be worn.

FIRST AID: Blood tests to be completed before ceremony. Gynaecologist to stand-by.

SOUND: Playback of 'Wedding March' and selections of Iolanthe and the Dubliners' greatest hits.

ANIMALS: Donkey races to be postponed until Sunday.

ELECTRICAL: Light change.

CONSTRUCTION: 6-inch pancake for groom.

ACCOUNTS: Please note pay cheques to be addressed in future to Mrs. Sheelagh Hippisley-Coxe.

TECHNICAL ADVISER: Patrick Stanley to be available if required.

DIALOGUE COACH: To rehearse groom on lines.

SCRIPT WRITER: Speeches to be delivered by 4.00.pm.

PLASTERERS: Wedding cake.

SECOND UNIT: To remain at Croc. Farm.

SFX: No gadgets required.

scouting the first shooting spot which was on the top of a nearby hill. Orders came down that they intended to shoot and presumably shoot the clouds away. As the trailer had not arrived there was nowhere for Colin, the comb and Paul, the sponge to work. Another order from the hill-top said we should take off back down the muddy track and use Jane's apartment at the Colony Hotel which was the nearest of those the unit is using for make-up and hair-dressing.

So off we went and had a pleasant respite from the wind and the rain while Paul patted pancake over my wrinkled sunburned chops. Paul had barely finished before Ray Becket, the Third Assistant, or 'Blade' as he has been dubbed because he is as lean as a piece of grass, was banging on the door to drag us back up the track and then to the hill-top.

The rest of the day we spend dodging out from the shelter of trees between showers to grab shots of Jimmy Bond and Solitaire searching for the secret of Kananga's wealth. The scenery from the four thousand foot high summit made it all worthwhile. A vast expanse of tall swaying sugar cane swept unbroken to the sea edge some five miles away.

Shooting in the rain reminded me of an episode on *Ivanhoe* when we filmed in soaking fields near Beaconsfield, Buckinghamshire. Like today, we waited for breaks in the weather and after three weeks of daily excursions to the quagmires without immortalizing the miserable scene, orders came from Columbia Pictures, 'Shoot it in the rain.' I donned my armour and the director, Lance Comfort, selected his camera angle and said 'Let's shoot.' As I clanked across to my position a strident voice strained through the drizzle:

'No, no, no, Mr Comfort, you can't shoot.'

It was my wardrobe master, a very chic ex-actor, John Briggs.

'Why not?' demanded the director.

'Well,' said John, taking a deep breath and fixing the

director's eyes with his own fervent gaze, 'his armour will get rusty.'

'Get stuffed,' said the director, and we swam our way into action.

B-Day Forty-five and back up the muddy track this morning after a night of bucketing rain. In today's sequence Jimmy Bond and Solitaire are spotted by Kananga's men and hide under the nets which camouflage the illicit poppy crop. A helicopter was hovering overhead which, on film, is the one Kananga's men bomb and fire at us from. We were to face special effects bangs, flashes and machine gun bullets for most of the day.

Jane knew that the bangs were coming but we did not warn her about the machine gun rattle so that the camera could capture her surprise. It worked. We hit the deck several times during the day but when the machine gun went off Jane bored into the mud like a bloody mole and managed to give herself a crack on the head with a blunt instrument, as they say. Full of sympathy, 'Crackers' came over and said:

'I hope the injury is something nasty, darling, so we can all have the day off.'

We had to do shot after shot and at one stage she was really scared. It was like being sent time after time to the dentists. In the script I hold her hand and I could feel her pulling back. We had to run through the poppy field and then into some ten foot sugar cane where I had told Jane there would be another explosion but I did not know the exact spot. We braced ourselves for the run in and the General called:

'Tear off. Action.'

We raced through and into the cane and nothing happened; the charge had not gone off, so back we went to begin again. We waited and Jane was tense. Then 'Crackers', who was part of the conspiracy, came up and said the trip wire to the explosive has got wet so we will forget that shot. Guy certainly got a fear-filled performance from Jane and she bore the bangs, flying mud and hot flashes like the professional she is and still looked lovely at the end of it.

It is wise to be wary of an over-enthusiastic special effects man. A film was being made about a British destroyer which heroically sailed through hellfire from Chinese shore batteries on the Yangtse. A special effects man managed to blow a bloody great hole in the side of the ship and stop it, which was more than the Chinese had managed to do.

We had a couple of minor casualties on the unit today. One was an Art Department man who I saw walking with his feet wide apart suffering from sweat rash on his backside and most private parts. He went to see the nurse who gave him a canister of alcohol to spray on it. He bent over and aimed the spray. It stung so much he took off like a launched rocket and banged his head on a bed-post. I had a similar experience when I was under contract to Warner Brothers. I had a lot of riding to do in a picture and on one particular day I must have been thrown half a dozen times. I went home bruised and aching and picked up some concoction at a drugstore which they said would take some of the ache and pain away. I had a long hot bath with salts which made me sweat then applied the substance to the bruised small of my back. The stuff mingled with sweat and trickled down past my rear end to my pride and joy. The pain was horrendous. I tried to wash it off with soap, then washing powder but with no effect. An hour later I called the doctor and he gave me an injection which knocked me out but it took twenty-four hours for the pain to go.

Today's other accident occurred to George Crawford who slipped on the mud, fell on his face and broke a tooth. He refused treatment and consoled himself with a bottle of Johnny Walker and will no doubt be back tomorrow merry and bright. George, who has one of the toughest jobs on the unit, is an ex-British Army Regimental Sergeant Major and his past dedication to discipline has come in handy here. From England there is only George and Tony Hardy, the cook, to cater for the unit of about a hundred and that number can swell to two hundred with drivers, labourers and extras. On arrival George recruited six Jamaican helpers who, he says, are now hard workers but were very raw. Pre-dawn punctuality is vital in George's job. Because of the early start to the working day in the film business hotels cannot be relied on to provide breakfast so it is served on the location site at anything from 5.30 AM. When the hungry horde does descend George must be ready or a king's ransom could be lost in shooting time.

The places breakfast must be served are as tricky as the timing. It might be a muddy hill-side, a swamp or a narrow side street. George's Jamaican helpers had no experience whatever of the film business and had never heard of location catering, so he began their training.

Unit punctuality begins with breakfast. George turns in to bed at about 9 PM, gets up at two-thirty every working morning and finishes sometimes at 7 PM. He is on his feet for sixteen hours almost without a break so his helpers came in for a shock. He broke them in by ordering a muster parade every morning at 6 AM. He stands them to attention best British infantry fashion and inspects their hands, nails and clothes for cleanliness. Then, just to make it abundantly clear that there will be no messing about, he takes them through ten minutes' drill. They march, wheel and mark time to George's barked orders. One morning he was so busy watching some frying fat that he nearly marched them over a twenty-foot drop.

Their first duty is to erect the tables and chairs on the location site and draw the water which feeds the chuck waggon, as the mobile cook-house is called. During the day they wait on tables, wash up or do a host of things that are necessary. Their last chore, sometimes at 6 PM is to clean the cook-house and leave the location site free from paper plates, cups and as clean as it was when the crew arrived.

Another of George's problems is controlling the drinks supply. He supplies soft drinks of several sorts; urns of tea, coffee, grapefruit and lime juice are on tap all day. Beer is available but, by company rule, only at lunchtime. So far, George has been threatened three times by Jamaican drivers and labourers for refusing to serve beer during working hours but Tony, George's cook, is a judo black belt holder and usually steps in to keep the complainants quiet.

B-Day Forty-six. Torrential rain this morning and I got a telephone call at my crack of dawn departure time from Ray, the Third Assistant, to say that the caravan had broken down so there would be nowhere for make-up and hairdressing to operate at the crocodile farm. Could I wait here at the villa and Paul, the make-up man, would come to me.

Ready, I arrived at the farm and dozed in the back of the car while we waited for the rain to stop. Julius, banging on the car window, broke my reverie; I had one minute to be in front of the cameras for the day's opening shot. That shows Jimmy Bond being bundled from a car past the 'Trespassers Will Be Eaten' sign, into the crocodile farm where, after some sadistic horseplay by Tee Hee and his hook, Bond is stranded on a bed-sized, knee-high island to be eaten by the crocs.

We were lining up the shot when there was a ripple in the water and Ross said we must move. It was a croc within striking distance and ready to tear someone's leg off. Ross stood on the retractable bridge which connects the small island with the land and dropped a hook on a heavy rope into the water. The croc, which was about fourteen feet long, bit and Ross whipped the rope around its mouth, then with the help of two of his men, hauled it close to the bank. Its tail was lashing like mad but he got on its back and began pressing it just behind the eyes which seemed to quieten it. Then he tied its forelegs and back legs with rope loops and wound another rope around its clamped jaw. Ross had asked for silence but the unit were all watching and someone spoke. 'Crackers' called for quiet but the General said he was ready to roll immediately. All told we lost an hour. The croc had to be heaved on a stretcher, then as the unit backed away, it was carried through them and put in a fenced pond two hundred yards away where Ross had to cut the ropes he had tied. He sharpened a knife on a stone, bound it to the end of a long stick then cut the bonds. The croc was not at all happy. He started snapping and thrashing and Ross beat a hasty retreat.

Julius went out on the small island where, as Tee Hee, he feeds the crocs more chicken with his pincers before leaving Bond there to be eaten. Suddenly there was another call from Ross Kananga.

'Hello, hello. I see one of my alligators is becoming very interested.'

Ross took off his shirt, stuck a revolver in his belt and waded through the muddy water, which has a high crocodile dung content, to a spot near an overhanging tree where he could keep a closer eye on the alligator and intercept it if it came nearer. When he was in position the crew moved a camera rest which had been set up in the water back on to land for the next shot.

The camera was on Julius feeding chicken to the crocs and Guy called 'Action'. Julius moved but his pincers wouldn't. It was stuck. 'Crackers' waded out through the slime to help him and came back. That was only the first of a string of snags which were to beset Julius. He had a lot of trouble timing his breathing so that his chest-operated hook would work and still look natural. At the same time he had to control his breath to deliver his dialogue which made it doubly difficult. It was baking hot and Julius got very upset. It took two hours and fifteen takes to get it right but on screen it will be seen in seconds.

Fire and thirteen hundred ferocious crocodiles made B-Day Forty-seven a day to remember and I am lucky to have lost no more than the hair on my hands and arms.

We shot the scene where Bond, encircled by crocodiles, escapes from the island near the shed where Kananga's workers are packing heroin. Bond surrounds the shed with benzine-soaked rags and rubber and lays a trail of chicken pieces from the swamp edge to the shed door. An alligator slithers from the swamp, follows the trail through a gate and inside the shed. The next thing we see are workers tumbling over each other to get out of the door on the other side, but Bond has lit the rags and ringed the building in flame.

To escape from the island Bond makes a death-defying leap over the crocodile infested water. I am glad we got this shot in the can quickly because I must confess my 'bottle' was twitching, which is a sure sign my adrenalin glands are working overtime. 'Bottle' for those unfamiliar with rhyming slang is short for 'bottle and glass' which rhymes with what was twitching.

When it came to flaming the rubber and rags round the building our Special Effects had a field day. The shed was circled in a sheet of fire and before I could dodge back the licking flames had singed all the hair off my hands and arms.

The whole thing went beautifully and our star alligator, dubbed Daisy, crawled on cue through the gate into the hut. Ross has had Daisy since she was eight and she is now thirty. From the moment he saw the *Live and Let Die* script Ross trained her to walk up the bank at a certain spot, choosing a nice, shady place she fancied and feeding her there. When Daisy was familiar with her walk the construction team then moved in and built the hut and gate at the end of it. Daisy is quite a tough lady; she is the alligator who killed two crocodiles and duffed up three more, loosing half her teeth in the conflict which upset Ross because she is not likely to grow any more. Personally, I am not at all perturbed.

In the film the crocodile swamp is not, of course, on San Monique but in Louisiana. After Bond fires the shed he belts away in a speed boat, which is why I was batting round the Louisiana bayous. In typical topsy-turvy film fashion we filmed Bond at the croc farm in Jamaica, jetting off in a boat to start the chase sequence we shot five weeks ago in Louisiana. The terrain of the crocodile farm in Jamaica and the bayous are strikingly similar, except for one thing: the depth of the water. The swamp water at its deepest is only two feet so, today, instead of zooming off in my jet boat I stuck in the mud and had to be pushed back to begin again. The work force dug channels where the water is sometimes only six inches deep but overnight the mud sank back.

The crocodiles and the boats are divided by stakes and very fine chicken wire through which eighty pairs of evil green eyes stare at us hungrily. I now know why it is called chicken wire; when you are on one side of it and the crocs are on the other you are very chicken.

Ross is suppose to clear the section where we are working each day but he has an unnerving habit of suddenly splashing into the water waving his pistol as he spies a maverick in the mud. Ask Ross why a certain croc is loose he says:

'Oh, that's dear old Daisy,' or, 'That's friendly Fred. I've had him for thirty years and he's all right.'

Before we began Ross moved ninety-six crocodiles from the area where we are working and he says he knows the exact number that lived there. But they burrow tunnels and stay submerged for months so I hope Ross has his arithmetic right and there is not the odd one basking below. The crocs have this petrifying practice of lurking log-like all day but moving imperceptibly nearer as the day wears on. As we finished today and 'Crackers' called: 'It's a wrap, fellows,' a log came alive and moved rapidly towards the cameras leaving a wake like the Queen Mary as if he said to himself: 'Christ! There goes my tea.'

Ross's pet is a personable one-year-old mongrel, half alsatian and half Rhodesian ridgeback – the African lion dog, blessed with the name Bullet. Bullet has lived in the swamp since he was seven weeks old and has an uncanny instinct for locating crocs. He swims about quite happily then suddenly freezes and Ross knows there is a scaly somewhere near. Bullet is too cocky with the crocs and Ross is worried that he will lose him. He would like a baby croc to nip him because he feels that until he gets hurt he will never learn crocodile caution. Bullet has had one narrow escape when Ross found him shaking and howling on a mud bank with a croc crashing its jaws a few feet away but it wasn't enough to scare some sense into him.

Our film shooting schedule is now clashing daily with the clock. After a lot of transatlantic telephone talking a Laker Airways DC 10 charter flight for England has been fixed for 20 December and before then we must have a clear day to pack our ten tons of equipment, plus personal belongings, and close the offices.

When I got home tonight I found a cable from my agent, Dennis Van Thal, about a script written by *Live and Let Die* writer, Tom Mankiewicz, which will be ready in the spring. I was sorry to see Tom leave New Orleans and thought he might be with us in Jamaica for additional writing, and he is. He is staying with Guy for a few days and it will be nice to see him again. I hoped Sidney Poitier and George Barrie, both of whom planned visits, would be with us but regrettably neither of them are going to make it.

Crying crocodile tears I said goodbye to my reptilian friends for today, B-Day Forty-eight, is our last day at the crocodile farm. It was with no exceptional sadness for I was not sorry to see their scaly backs; they are nasty, smelly, jagged-teeth beasts. Mosquitoes are quite nice by comparison. A sad thing about the movie business is that holidays, Christmas included, must go by the board when necessary. The second unit of four, in the charge of Nick Hippisley-Coxe, are staying through Christmas and the New Year to shoot crocodile close-ups, and best of British luck. With them will be the location manager, Bernard Hanson, who has already been here a lot longer than most of us. Nick has his new wife, Sheelagh, to keep him company and a couple of the other fellow's wives are flying out to spend the Christmas holidays on the beach in eighty degrees of heat while the rest of us shiver back in England. While we are dreaming of a white Christmas, Nick dreams of crocodiles. He has now worked in the swamp for several weeks while the first unit has been shooting on other locations and crocodiles have crept into his subconscious. When Nick told Ross that he dreamt he was sharing his bridal bed with Bongos, the killer croc, and Sheelagh, Ross told us of the night he fell asleep embracing a local lovely. In a nightmare soft skin turned to scales and as she turned into a croc Ross tipped her out of bed and they both woke as he bounded backwards across the room. He had a terrible time explaining to the bewildered girl that he dreamt he was wrestling with a crocodile.

Ross's life and work is so interwoven with crocs it is not surprising that he dreams about them. He has even said he can think of worse ways to die than be eaten by them and a few days ago, under the helpless gaze of the second unit, he nearly was. Stepping from the small island he trod on a crocodile's back, his foot slipped off into its open jaws and for a terrifying moment he was seconds away from death with no time to reach for the gun at his hip. Nick Hippisley-Coxe hopes he never witnesses anything like it again. 'We were completely helpless,' he told me. 'We could do nothing. If he had been caught he would certainly have lost a limb, if not his life.'

But Ross Kananga could not live with the thought of dying over a desk as he filled in insurance forms. A drop-out from a Cornell University business administration course he chose to make a living riding wild bulls in South American rodeos before coralling crocodiles. The necklace of curved crocodile teeth he wears round his neck proclaims a predilection for a life style which demands that he lives dangerously or not at all.

Today the wooden hut housing the heroin was set on fire and I could not resist teasing Ross who takes everything I say seriously. We shot the surrounding circle of fire yesterday and today we filmed the fire licking the wood of the hut as workers rush from the door. On film it will look as though the shed goes up in flames but in reality the fire was spaced so that the building was left virtually intact. I make my motor boat escape while the inferno rages behind me.

The fire brigade was hidden out of sight down the road and 'Crackers' warned them they would be needed at any time and must keep their equipment and water pressure ready for instant use. The flames were leaping and 'Crackers' called them. Somehow they had let one of the heavy's cars we use in the scene block the road between the fire engine and the blaze. The car had to reverse back into the flames so that the fire engine could inch past. Hoses at the ready, they stood while we waited with bated breath for the deluge to flood the flames. The pressure was down and out of the hose came a trickle. For seconds the fireman holding it stood like a four-year-old shaking the drips off his willy. Ross, who was watching, got very agitated because he hopes to turn the shed, which is about sixty feet by forty feet, into a restaurant and he was promised it would be left standing. I told him the whole thing was going up in smoke and he could forget any ideas he might have for it. His face dropped and he kept saying: 'Jesus! But they said they were gonna leave it!'

Just then the fire brigade got their pressure up and streams of water soon had the fire out. Ross looked relieved until I told him they had only put it out so we could blow it up. He began to look really mad and I thought he was going to call up his crocs so I hastily told him I was joking.

Today we also shot a scene where Bond stands on the tiny island throwing chicken pieces to the crocs to keep them at bay. We discovered that the fridge had been left off overnight and the meat had gone putrid. It stank so much I could hardly handle it and in any case the crocs wouldn't eat it. 'Crackers' ' beady eyes fell on neatly severed portions of fowl George Crawford was preparing.

'But it's for the unit lunch,' wailed George.

'This is an emergency,' said 'Crackers', sternly.

'The pieces are too small,' said George, triumphantly.

'Sew 'em up again, then,' suggested 'Crackers'.

And they did. The crocodiles got trussed chicken, which they ate with evident enjoyment, while the unit had a scratch lunch.

An early finish to the day and nothing more to do but bid farewell to our only friend in the swamps, Ross. We left him waving goodbye at the gate of his grisly farm, his teeth, both his own and the crocodiles round his neck, gleaming and his gun butt protruding from his belt. A truly remarkable man.

B-Day Forty-nine. It has been a series of lasts all day. The last shot of the location, a bungalow exterior at Half Moon Bay, five miles from the villa, where I walk on to the veranda for breakfast and call for Rosie. We had set up, shot and wrapped long before lunch and our work here was over. It was a last minute packing and last minute shopping day for Luisa in which I refused to be involved and my last of so many location photo sessions. It was with Oscar Abolafia of Transworld Features who had waited patiently

125

for days while I worked at the crocodile farm where photographers were forbidden. With several other photographic situations Oscar had me sitting on the beach in my location chair which has 007 emblazoned on the back and staring King Canute-like defiantly at the sea.

Poor General Hamilton who has beaten tropical torrents to finish location filming before Christmas was himself beaten by the rain on his first rest day for two months. He was looking forward to a game of golf on the course which spreads tantalizingly below his villa overlooking the sea, but if he had played today he would have needed a snorkel and flippers. Tom Mankiewicz and I went down to the club and had a few commiserating bloody marys with him.

It seems an eternity yet no time at all since we started shooting in New Orleans. There is so much to remember; I can still hear the music of the jazz funeral and I will long listen to the echo of the early birds singing at Ocho Rios. I will remember many friendly faces, people's kindness and their cooperation.

A black faced Father Christmas in a red robe, sweating under his white wool beard in Montego Bay's steamy main street this afternoon did nothing to persuade me that Christmas is coming. But it is, and Luisa is adding to our twenty-four pieces of luggage (only two of which are mine) with Christmas gifts. The children are looking forward to going home to the pony and the dog; I am looking forward to Sunday papers, English marmalade, frosty mornings and seeing my mother and father. What I am not looking forward to is seeing Gatwick Airport at 4.30 in the morning!

Suspense of a different sort. Everyone is packed and ready for the flight home; the plane is here but cannot take off. A 345 seat Laker Airways DC10, it has developed a fault in the undercarriage hydraulics and we have to wait for a part to be flown from England. Take off time should have been 1 PM today but it now looks like being midnight at the earliest and more likely much later.

Worse, injury caught up with us in the last twenty-four hours of the location. George Crawford fell from the catering truck and had nine stitches in his hand. Gordon Gowing, one of the electricians, is in hospital with concussion after slipping from another truck and could be unfit to fly with us, while Bill Nunn of the Special Effects department will be hobbling aboard with the aid of walking sticks after a rolling gas cylinder broke his toe.

Airborne at last after a seventeen hour delay, today began by being 'In Bond' day. The call came for us to be at Montego Bay Airport at 5.30 AM for our ten hour flight. We converged on the airport in two coaches and nine cars from the villas and hotels we have occupied. After half an hour's wait the Bonded Store at the airport opened for us to collect about five thousand pounds' worth of duty free shopping the crew had done in Montego Bay.

The wait was a nervous one for the unit. The delay could easily have caused confusion among the scattered duty free shops in Montego Bay who cannot by law hand the goods over the shop counter but must deliver them to the airport Bond Store for handover at the time of the customer's take-off. But no one knew, until that last minute, what time we would take off. Had the goods been delivered for the first take-off time and returned to the shops? If not, were they behind the closed shutters of the Bonded Store? We chatted the minutes away until six AM then the roller shutters raised. Receipts fluttered and in a few minutes the departure lounge had transformed into a bumper birthday party with everyone bursting open cartons, parcels and packets to check their buys. The place filled with the sounds of new stereo equipment, radios and the click and whirr of new cine and stills cameras. With those, the watches, clocks, the excess whisky and tobacco, British Customs will have a ball.

Another delay while our luggage and ten tons of equipment was loaded and we were away. Eighty-eight of us, including wives, children and all injured with three hundred and forty-five seats to spread over. The Jamaican coastline fell away and so did the murky green patch which marked the crocodile farm. Two of the crew each stretched over four seats and promptly fell asleep. One was a bearded unit member who caught the plane with seconds to spare after a hectic last night with a lively lady American schoolteacher. The other was Jane Oscroft, the hard-working production secretary. Jane, who on the face of it has a job with its film glamour and foreign travel that thousands of girls might envy, is returning home just as pale as she came but much more exhausted after working over twelve hours a day seven days a week in the production office with barely time to see a beach, much less sunbathe.

After breakfast the children and some of the adults watched a screening of *The Railway Children* before we began to lose height for a refuelling touchdown in Newfoundland. There could hardly have been a greater contrast in climate and countryside between the one we had just left and the snow-swept plains and leafless black fir forests which lifted towards us as we landed.

A sub-zero blast swept through the open plane doors and many of the unit who were wearing only lightweight clothes wrapped themselves in Laker Airways bright yellow blankets for a quick shuddering dash to the shops in the air terminal.

Back aboard we drank, talked and sang our way across the Atlantic. At Gatwick Airport we flew through barely passable fog to land in the dark. It was cold and damp. Icy mist issued forth from our freezing lips as we descended the plane's steps; but what the hell! It's home . . . and Christmas.

*   *   *

B-Day Fifty and back to work after the Christmas holidays. It was a bit like the first day of term at Pinewood Studios as I discovered my dressing room and located make-up and hairdressing. The unit were all muffled up against the early morning cold; their Jamaican tans already beginning to fade. Paul Rabiger was wearing trousers, instead of the frayed denim shorts he has worn for months.

It was a pleasant restful Christmas. At 10 AM the morning after our arrival from Jamaica I woke to an English breakfast, and by 12 NOON Luisa and I were having our yuletide argument in Hamley's in Regent Street about what Father Christmas was going to bring the children. After an hour of getting jostled to death in the toy shop we went on to the hallowed hush of Asprey's where I didn't get jostled to death but my wallet did. At Harrods we saw friendly faces; among them Kirk Douglas's wife, Anne, and producer Jay Kanter. It was a day of surprises; I even saw a lady in Harrods without a fur coat!

Cooking Christmas dinner is my speciality and I do it every year, so Fortnum and Masons was our next stop for firm brussels sprouts, jars of Stilton cheese and all the little delicacies which make my English Christmas. We saw more friends and fellow actors in Fortnums and not all of them being served; some were serving. If my son wants to be an actor I won't bother to send him to drama school to get the right accent; I'll just let him serve at Fortnums for a few months. That is, if I can afford the tailcoat.

My children, still suffering from the five hour Jamaican time lag, did not wake at six AM on Christmas morning like I used to, but at 9 AM thank God! Then we had great excitement while they opened their presents. David Tebet, Vice-President of NBC, was our house guest. If he doesn't spend Christmas with us he goes to Hawaii. If I were he I would rather go to Hawaii. We were joined for Christmas lunch by Kirk Douglas, who is making a musical version of Dr Jekyll and Mr Hyde for television at Shepperton Studios, and his wife, Anne. Their children are in California and they were missing them sadly over Christmas. With Vic Heutschy, the American publicist, his wife Elly, David, my mother and father, Luisa and I and the children, we were eleven round the table and a very happy party. I popped over to see Harry, who lives close, to wish him a happy Christmas and we also saw Michael Caine and Shakira and were delighted with the news of their forthcoming nuptials.

Christmas began to recede and Jamaica seemed even further away as I came on to 'A' stage this morning where the inside of Bond's hotel bungalow has been built. He has just been told by the reception clerk that 'Mrs Bond' awaits him there and discovers Rosie Carver. I did not discover Rosie Carver, however, this morning, as I was the only member of the cast who worked today. I won't be working with my lovely leading ladies for a few days.

Tonight we are going to David Tebet's birthday party. The year before last I threw a big party for his birthday and this year Kirk and Anne Douglas are doing the honours at their London home, in South Eaton Place. The house belongs to George Axelrod who is living in Kirk and Anne's Palm Springs home while he is in California.

B-Day (or Bidet) Fifty-one was bath day for Bond, who, settled into his hotel bungalow, decides to shave while soaking in the suds. As he gets in the bath the audience sees a serpent sliding down a pipe to attack his hind quarters; but before it can strike someone enters the bungalow and Bond leaps out of the bath.

Our snake, imported from Florida, should have arrived today for the scene but it had not cleared customs. Ever tried searching a snake for smuggled pot? We could shoot some of the scene without my sinuous supporting star but I shall have to get back in the bath on Monday to complete the sequence.

When ladies do a bath scene they have a closed set and nobody is allowed on, but with me, everybody and his auntie came on and modesty apart, every time someone opened the door a vicious north-westerly draught cooled my bubble bath. If I didn't catch pneumonia leaping about in a draught soaking wet I was in severe danger of electrocution from all the lights, cables and plugs surrounding my slopping bath water. It was freeze to death or frizzle to death. Ah, well. Bond lives dangerously.

Last night I was doing another kind of soaking at a marvellous party Kirk and Anne gave for David Tebet. Harry and Jackie were there and it was nice to see other old friends like Sir Lew and Lady Grade, the Jay Kanters and Joan Collins and her husband Ron Kass. We met a very pretty girl, Lesley Anne Down, who is in *Scalawag*, Anne Douglas's first picture as a producer.

After a day in the bath, my face covered in lather, I was cleaner than I have ever been in my life; I had used three pots of shaving cream and my skin was beginning to wrinkle like a prune. When I got home dear Luisa, with my best interests at heart, said she had prepared just the thing to relax me before dinner – a nice hot bath.

B-Day Fifty-two. Glory Ass came back to us, my solo act ended and I got a few lines of dialogue to say. It makes a change from squeezing a sponge. Not a very nice welcome back for Gloria as in our first scene I had to throw her across the room. As Rosie Carver she creeps into Bond's bungalow in the dark, he thinks it is somebody after him and spins her across the room on to a convenient bed. Gloria sailed through the air, losing none of her grace and managing to land in a very feminine way.

Today, somewhat excited, I saw myself as Bond for the first time in a few feet of rushes and as I hadn't seen a foot of film since we started shooting it was quite a tense moment for me. A sort of teaser trailer of the film has been put together and shown in cinemas over Christmas both here and in America. Five hundred were printed for America and the exhibitors were so pleased they ordered another three hundred. There are two hundred going round in England.

Harry says we are going to do the same sort of thing again at Easter. The build-up of publicity and advertising for the film is fascinating. I was asking Harry about the sort of money the Bonds have made in the past and he told me the biggest grosser was *Thunderball* which has done 64 million dollars to date. *Diamonds are Forever*, the last before *Live and Let Die*, has already grossed 48 million and it is only on its first time round. *OHMSS* was the lowest and even that grossed 25 million dollars. I just hope ours will be as successful. Derek Coyte told me the première will probably be the first week in July in England and in America, too, where 4th July is a big holiday weekend. We are hoping for Royalty at our première in London.

Being back at Pinewood I am seeing a lot of old mates. I had a long laugh with Frankie Howerd at lunchtime and a chat with director Don Chaffey. I was very pleased to hear that Don is making a picture at Pinewood with Lana Turner who will arrive in a few days. Lana starred in the first film in which I had my name above the title – *Diane*. She asked what else was shooting at Pinewood and they told her the Bond film. She was reportedly delighted and said:

'Ah. Roger is in that.'

I am flattered that she does, at least, remember me.

I had a very special lady to lunch today, my daughter, Deborah, who told me when she grew up she was going to take over from me, I could retire and she would keep me. I don't quite see her as 007 but she seems keen to get her screen career started. She stood, hugging my hand, by the side of the set and whispered up to me:

'Can't we go on the set and do a real movie kiss?'

* * *

New Year's B-Day Fifty-three and Pinewood in the grip of heavy fog nudged nostalgia for the swamps, the mosquitoes, the humidity and the crocodiles. Yesterday I drove to Marlow for a New Year's Eve lunch at the Compleat Angler and got lost on what should have been a twenty minute drive home on a road I know backwards.

Luisa and I gave a New Year's Eve dinner party and brought Bond birds past and present together; Jane was with her husband, Michael Attenborough, and Shirley Eaton with her husband, Colin Rowe. Nobody who saw *Goldfinger* can forget Shirley, glistening gold paint on every inch of her naked body, sprawled on a bed, beautiful but dead. Derek and Julie Cracknell completed our dinner party. My New Year resolution, in spite of my last New Year resolution never to make another, is to get New Year's Day as a public holiday. Nobody works except the English and as today we become members of the Common Market it is high time we happily conformed with the continent. I tried to persuade Harry to set the trend and give us a holiday New Year's Day but no such luck. At my little dinner party we managed to sink an awful lot of champagne, red wine and port and I, in common with most of the crew, felt delicate this morning. Only the snake had the good sense to take the day off. It is still on its way. Baths, I bear witness, are no hangover cure. I was back in the one on the stage at 8.30 AM for the first half-a-dozen hot dips for the scene where I dash from the bath to the door.

The Studio, closed all over the weekend, was icy this morning and jumping in and out of a hot bath and running around in a bath robe I was freezing to bloody death. After indulging myself over Christmas and New Year I am watching my diet and planned skipping lunch but I was shivering so much I ordered a bowl of soup. The 'soup of the day' in English film studios is really the 'soup of the week' because the kidney soup I got at lunchtime will be on the menu as Brown Windsor tomorrow, on Wednesday they will put a carrot in it and call it vegetable, on Thursday a leak and it's cock-a-leekie and on Friday they will dye it white and call it cream of mushroom.

Today Gloria and I continued the bungalow scene and it took twelve takes to get the shot in the can. Gloria is an actress who relates dialogue to her own experiences and something about saying the word 'useless' really bugged her and the line would not come right. To be fair, Gloria did not blow all twelve takes herself; one was my fault and the camera blew a couple. In the scene, double agent Rosie, having been thrown on the bed by Bond, loses her wig, goes into the bathroom to put it back on, sees the snake and rushes out screaming. She tells Bond: 'It's no good I shouldn't have gotten into this in the first place. I am completely useless.'

Ad libbing without a flicker of a leer on my face, I looked her straight in the eye and said:

'Don't worry, darling. We'll soon lick you into shape. It's getting late.'

To my horror Tom Mankiewicz walked on set just as I was re-writing his scene. I felt as though I had changed *Hamlet* in front of William Shakespeare. Tom felt the line was too crude but I cracked we would put a footnote on the credits: 'Screenplay. Tom Mankiewicz. One line of additional dialogue by Roger Moore.'

On Friday night we at last managed to catch the Anthony Newley and Leslie Brictsse show *The Good Old Bad Old Days* which opened while we were in Jamaica. Kirk and Anne Douglas were to have accompanied Harry and Jackie and Luisa and me, but at the last minute Kirk had to cancel because of make-up tests on *Dr Jekyll and Mr Hyde*. The rest of us arrived at the theatre in Harry's enormous Rolls-Royce E O N 1 (named after the company) to confront a crowd of cameramen expecting to get snaps of Spartacus and James Bond together. They were rather disappointed and so were the show's cast who had been looking forward to meeting Kirk. We were fêted splendidly with champagne after what was a superb show and I don't say that because I have a little money in it; it really is first class.

Afterwards we went to Drones for dinner where the walls are covered with pictures of film stars as babies. Everybody has been approached from Noel Coward to Natalie Wood and mine is next to a lady I have worshipped since I first saw her on the set of *Perfect Strangers* when she was the star and I was a sixteen-year-old extra in a sailor's uniform. There she sat at the next table and although I had never spoken to her in my life, our baby photos hanging cheek by jowl gave me the perfect opportunity to introduce myself to the delightful Deborah Kerr.

B-Day Fifty-four.

'Now, if he should bite and lock his teeth for God's sake don't jerk away.'

The 'he' in question was a particularly ugly, unpleasant three foot long snake and the advice came from his handler. I can't bring myself to say trainer because this reptile was not even house-broken, let alone trained.

'Why shouldn't I jerk?' I inquired, swallowing nervously.

'You'll pull his teeth out,' said the handler.

'Sod his teeth,' I yelled. 'What about his poison!'

'He's of a non-venomous variety,' I was told.

'Does he know that?' I queried.

What a conversation for 8.30 in the morning. This is not going to be one of my good days, I thought to myself, wishing I was back in the bath.

There I was, barefooted, offering a tempting target to this refugee from a shoe factory. Endeavouring to look relaxed, nonchalant and generally Bondy, I lit my Monte Cristo Especial and slipped my gold Dunhill back into my dressing-

135

gown pocket. The camera panned down on my hand and continued on to the bath mat where my serpentine co-star slithered, darting its long forked tongue in my direction. Disposing of this little scene stealer was the best part of the day but I am not going to give the game away and say how 007 foils the fangs.

A little light has gone out of our lives with the leaving of lovely Gloria who has completed her scenes here and gone off on an Austrian holiday where her warm exuberance is probably melting the mountain snows. She is quite a girl; she endeared herself to the whole unit, and for myself, I couldn't have wished for a more delightful double agent to trigger my career in the Secret Service. Gloria's goodbye will be marked in my mind by a letter which arrived today from a lady in North Wales who had seen Gloria and myself pictured as a bridal pair in the *Daily Express*.

The lady prefixed her comments with the point that Enoch Powell was her favourite Member of Parliament, then proceeded:

Oh, how could you do such a thing? I have been a fan of yours since the first episode of the Saint and to me you were the perfect specimen of what a well-groomed Englishman should look like. To see you arm in arm with a black woman made me shudder and other silly men looking at the photograph will think it doesn't matter to marry a black and so produce half-breed children. I know it was only for a film but please don't do it again.

I wonder if you realize that England is well on the way to being a practically black nation as many towns already have more blacks than whites. Birmingham already I am told that white people are already in the minority. A surgeon friend of mine who lives there as I once did, said to a black nurse in a hospital 'I don't know what we should do without you.' Her reply was 'When we are strong enough we will split your throats.' This is perfectly true as my friend before retirement was well known in the hospitals. I guess your nice wife didn't like at all the photo in the Express *of 11 December. Don't please be photographed again.*

B-Day Fifty-five was a dizzy day; I spent it in a revolving restaurant booth. The sequence takes place at the beginning of *Live and Let Die* when Bond is in New York, which perversely will be our last location sometime in February when we finish at Pinewood. Bond has followed Mr Big's heavies to his Harlem hideout, named like its New Orleans counterpart The Fillet of Soul. He is shown to a side booth table and before he can touch the drink he orders, the wall slides back and the booth with Bond inside swings round on a pivot depositing him before Mr Big in a secret back room. Waiters in restaurants where Harry habitually sends back the food might take to the idea and fit the same sort of tables.

Yaphet Kotto, our Mr Big, has joined us and we are working together for the first time, although we met on several occasions when he came to New Orleans and Jamaica for make-up tests. I am not surprised he needed so many tests; his make-up takes anything from three to four hours in the chair. I usually rehearse while he is being made-up but sometimes he has to get out of the chair before he is finished so I can get in it.

We said goodbye to our six foot three inches tall Texan special photographer, John Bryson in Jamaica and have now been joined at Pinewood by his British equivalent, the five foot, five inches, laconic, likeable Cockney, Terry O'Neill. Today Terry asked me if I would go with Gloria to the house of Vic Lowndes, Playboy Club boss in Britain, to do some pictures.

'What sort of pictures?' I asked.

'Nude pictures,' said Terry.

'Now, look here,' I expostulated, 'I've told you I don't strip off for *Cosmopolitan* and I won't do it for *Playboy*, either. It's one of the things I draw the line at and its not my scene at all.'

'No, no. It's Gloria who will be in the nude. You'll be fully dressed,' he soothed.

'And so will Luisa with a meat cleaver in her hand,' I replied.

'Oh,' said Terry, disappointed, 'does that mean you won't do it?'

It most certainly did mean I wouldn't do it. I reckon if you are pictured with a gun in your hand you should look as though you are going to use it and if you've got something else in your hand you should look as though you mean to use that, too, and I have no intention of standing there looking lifeless with a naked lady.

Tonight was 'best man and brides' night; Kenny More, who was my best man as I was his, and our brides, Angela and Luisa, got together for a very pleasant reunion dinner. Luisa and I had something else to celebrate, too. The Moore ménage is expecting an addition. The doctor confirmed it to Luisa today; no doubt about it, I am to become a father again. Luisa doesn't want it announced yet because of the fuss and possible barrage of Press calls, but we won't be able to resist telling a few friends.

Believe it or not, a day off. I have a sneaking suspicion they may be shooting tests of a replacement for me!

Every year Leslie Grade treats my family to the Royal Box at the London Palladium for the pantomime but today Geoffrey put this year's visit in jeopardy by developing raging toothache. We got him to our dentist and friend, Rene Karat, and of course by the time we arrived the tooth had miraculously stopped aching. Rather than spoil the afternoon for Geoffrey, Rene gave him some soluble aspirin and made an appointment for tomorrow to have the tooth out under anaesthetic.

Edward Woodward and Derek Nimmo in *Babes in the Wood* took Geoffrey's mind off his tooth all afternoon, but at eight o'clock tonight back came the toothache and the tears. My dentist, Rene, and Dr Roach, my anaesthetist, were dragged away from their dinner tables and by 9.30 PM Geoffrey was in the dentist chair with me acting as nurse. Three minutes and two molars later it was all over but as they removed the swabs Geoffrey's very wobbly front tooth got knocked out. Poor little thing. He half woke up and still in a trance kept saying:

'Where are my teeth? Where are my teeth?'

Still, I'm glad he didn't miss the pantomime because as well as the Royal Box we got the treatment to go with it and Deborah said she felt like Princess Anne standing there when they played the 'Queen'. I told her I had actually worn a crown while sitting in the same Royal Box years ago when I was to compère *Sunday Night at the London Palladium* for an American television special. Each special had a different compère and the week before my show it was Lorne Green. As a sort of trailer I was shown in the audience of his show sitting in the Royal Box wearing a crown.

B-Day Fifty-six. One more day shooting Bond falling for Mr Big's tricks. This time Bond sits at a restaurant table which suddenly sinks through the floor and deposits him, still in his chair, at Mr Big's feet in another secret hideaway, where Tee Hee, watched by Solitaire, manacles him to a chair.

I went along to rushes and discovered that in my absence yesterday they used the feet of my stand-in, John Woods, for a shot with the snake. To my horror, he is totally flat-footed. When I tackled him he said,

'Oh, yes. I nearly got drummed out of the Army because of it. That's why I was in the Cavalry.'

Talking of feet reminds me of a ticklish incident when I was in *Mr Roberts* at the London Coliseum. The late Tyrone

Power was playing the lead and in one scene Mr Roberts has coerced the Captain into giving the ship's crew liberty. As the announcement is made from the bows of the ship the sailors are heard happily singing 'Roll Me Over in the Clover'. To get this effect the whole cast of fifty, most of them stuntmen playing husky American sailors, were bunched unseen behind the tiny set of the ship's bows in the dark at the back of the stage. They were all big fellows and clumsy, too, so Ty suggested their shuffling presence would be less obvious if they took their shoes off. The first night we tried it some joker scattered tintacks and instead of 'Roll me Over in the Clover' came 'Ouch!' 'Ow!' 'OO!' as we jumped up and down in the dark in our stockinged feet. Then quite distinctly, said Ty later, came a strong indignant stage whisper which the audience must have heard:

'What bastard put these down?'

We have been rejoined by our second unit back from Jamaica, the crocodiles and a wet, rainy Christmas. After we left it poured incessantly and it was so cold they had to keep their coats on. A turkey famine hit the island and it was only by putting pleading pressure on the Half Moon Hotel to find them a turkey that they got their Christmas dinner. None of them fancied the local speciality saltfish and ackee as a substitute.

They are all glad to be home except Nick Hippisley-Coxe who is missing his favourite alligator. Some of Ross Kananga's enthusiasm for the brutes has rubbed off on Nick. He told me:

'I quite fancied this girl alligator. I thought she was very pretty. Whenever we got the cameras out she would come swimming up from the other end of the pond as if to say good morning. She was never frightened by all the commotion; the others would splash off when something disturbed them but she would stay and swim around.'

Nick became very attached to a six-inches-long baby crocodile called 'Captain Morgan' which the unit adopted

140

and fed sardines. Ross kept him in a tank and the moment anyone from the unit came near, Captain Morgan would jump up for a sardine. He was hatched from an egg Ross sent to Windsor Safari Park near London and in July Ross will bring him back for a visit. Nick has invited Captain Morgan to stay in his bath tub but is meeting with opposition from Sheelagh who doesn't fancy having her back scratched by a baby crocodile.

In Africa alone crocodiles consume well over a thousand people every year and to put Nick off his man-eating mates I told him the story related by a Pinewood Studio staff man who is a veteran of the Burma Campaign in World War II. The British Army had driven about a thousand Japanese infantrymen into a mangrove swamp on the Bay of Bengal. The Japanese Navy were unable to penetrate a British naval blockade to rescue their soldiers. Darkness fell and the swamp stirred alive with crocodiles. The sailors on the British ships helplessly listened to the night-long cries of men being eaten alive. Of the thousand soldiers who sought shelter in the swamp only twenty survived the night.

When Yaphet Kotto came to New Orleans and gave the Black Power salute there were those who said he had a chip on his shoulder. As a black actor in a predominantly white industry perhaps he believed he had to assert himself. One thing I do know is that he need have no chip on his shoulder about his acting ability because today he showed himself to be an actor of extraordinary depth and power. Today was not B-Day 57 but K for Kotto Day.

The scene between Bond and Mr Big in his hideout was a complicated one with many camera moves and ran for four minutes which is a long time in movie terms. Inevitably a scene of this length is carried by one actor and in this case it was Yaphet. My part called only for the odd interjection. For me this is worse because when the scene is going well I sit and sweat hoping I won't blow it when it comes to my line. Yaphet was magnificent, pulling all sorts of tricks out of his bag that he hadn't shown in rehearsal and I was so open-mouthed at his performance I did what I dreaded I would do and blew my tag line.

At the end of the scene Tee Hee taps Bond on the head with his metal hand, Bond slumps unconscious and a character called Whisper, played by Earl Jolly Brown, picks up his inert body under one arm and carries him out like a sack of cement. Earl weighs 295 lbs and to help his one-arm lift I wear a harness under my jacket with a handle so he can get a good grip. In spite of this he followed me around all morning eyeing my 175 lbs speculatively and suggesting I give lunch a miss.

He stuck close to the tea trolley and glared at me every time I reached for a bun or a cup of tea. Jane had very little to do in the scene except look beautiful in a brocade hand-painted crimson costume designed by Julie Harris. When Jane walked on set the dress had a quite modest, or as the weathermen say, a cool front. Before the first shot the front had become distinctly warmer; it was opened up exposing us to considerable cleavage that will no doubt delight the audience as much as it did the rest of us. She had only one line to say in the whole scene but breathed life into her part, you might say.

And so to bed, where I will spend most of the next twenty-four hours. Tonight with my lovely Luisa and to-morrow with Jane, surrounded by lights, cameras and a small army of technicians when we shoot our love scene.

I was in bed with my leading lady when Princess Alexandra's sister-in-law telephoned.

'Oh, dear,' said the Hon Mrs June Ogilvy, 'I do hope I am not disturbing you.'

'Not at all,' I hastened to assure her. 'I am only deflowering

Solitaire.' And I was, for B-Day Fifty-eight was my big love scene with Jane. Despite the fact that her father-in-law Richard Attenborough, is one of my best friends and her husband has had dinner at our house it was still an enjoyable experience, even if she was wearing thick tights and knickers under her flimsy negligee! It reminded me of something Joan Collins said when she came to lunch on Sunday with her husband, Ron Kass. Doing a love scene with a leading man she detested she armed herself with tights and the heaviest pair of football socks she could find. She didn't say which club's socks she wore but if Jane had turned up in football socks they would doubtless have been Chelsea since her father-in-law is Chairman of the Club. Jane, cuddling a hot water bottle between takes, complained of the cold but stoically reminded herself it was all in a good cause.

And that is what the Hon Mrs June Ogilvy was telephoning me about; a good cause. She is President of the Stars Organization for Spastics of which I am Chairman. The charity première of *Live and Let Die* was to have been exclusively in aid of the National Playing Fields Association and as Chairman of SOS it was a slight embarrassment that the proceeds from my most important picture should go to another charity. To try and resolve that Graham Dowson, Deputy Chief Executive of the Rank Organization, with a little push from Sir James Carreras, recently retired head of Hammer Films, lunched with June Ogilvy and our secretary, Sheila Rawsthorne. I learned the result last night as we sat round the dining table in the boardroom at Rank Headquarters in South Street as twenty of us, who had gathered to discuss the première, ploughed our way through sole bonne femme and rack of lamb. Twenty-five per cent of the première's proceeds will go to SOS and as we hope the première will raise forty or fifty thousand pounds it will mean a tidy sum for needy spastics. The première will now be somewhere between 9 and 12 July, depending on the availability of a Royal personage.

Luisa complains that we always go out with other people and never just on our own so we had an evening at the pictures and a cosy dinner for two tonight. We went to see Sean Connery in *The Offence* and thoroughly enjoyed it. It's a splendid film with great performances from Sean, Ian Bannen and Trevor Howard.

I telephoned Sean afterwards to tell how much we enjoyed it and how good it was. He has been so kind and complimentary to me and to Guy that it was nice to return the compliment; an easy task since the film really was excellent.

We followed the cinema with a romantic dinner at a favourite restaurant of ours, the Osteria San Lorenzo in Beauchamp Place, one of the best Italian restaurants in London. Lorenzo and his wife Mara run it superbly and have been friends of ours for years. Mara joined us for a drink and entertained us with hysterically funny stories of how people behave in restaurants. Last night an American lady with four children ordered first courses of spaghetti followed by huge steaks. Having eaten antipasto, then big platefuls of spaghetti the children hardly touched the steaks and the American lady called a waiter over and asked for a 'doggy bag' to take the rest away. At this point one of the kids piped up loudly:

'Gee, mommy, we don't have a dog.'

B-Day Fifty-nine. I got out of bed, did my work-out, had a shower, had a shave, brushed my teeth, got dressed, ate my breakfast scrambled eggs, got into the car, drove to the studio, took my clothes off and got back into bed with Jane Seymour. It's a hell of a way to earn a living! Picking up the passion where we dropped it at 5.30 yesterday afternoon is no joke at 8.30 in the morning when your hands are freezing cold and your toes like ice, but that is what picture acting is all about.

Jane warned me before we started shooting that she was

a giggler. She managed to restrain her humour in the bed scene but later in the day when we had a scene together in the cabin of Quarrel's boat which has been reconstructed on the set, it all got too much for her. The scene takes place after Bond has bedded Solitaire and as a tag I feed Jane the line: 'Where would you like to go.' Her reply, as she leans seductively back patting the bunk beside her, is:

'Anywhere where there is one of *these.*'

She managed her part all right without breaking up, although she once inadvertently said, 'Anywhere where there is one of *those,*' which broke everybody else up. I innocently asked, 'Is that where the expression bunk-up came from,' which didn't help and to make matters worse the cabin was rebuilt on springs and bounced up and down by burly prop men to simulate a sea sway. When it came to my close-ups Jane couldn't contain herself and everytime I gazed at her romantically she burst into giggles. In the end Guy sent her off the set in disgrace like a naughty schoolgirl.

I tried playing the line to one of the sparks but as I gazed at the stubble on his chin I realized it would not work. So I looked deep into his ear 'ole and with deep conviction said: 'It's only a case of heroin smuggling. I'll have a word with a man called Leiter. I'll turn the case over to him and then you and I will go off. Where would you like to go?'

The sparks never did tell me where he would like to go but as his ear 'ole didn't giggle we finally got the scene in the can.

We were wrong to fool around and I apologized to Guy who was rightly angry. Before shooting began I dropped him a note telling him to kick me up the backside if I got out of line and I invited him to do just that today.

B-Day Sixty – a slow day with nothing much to do but play practical jokes on Yaphet Kotto. It started a few days ago when Yaphet, came in one morning absolutely furious with a black singer he had seen on television the night before who he said had dyed his hair blond. Yaphet made cutting quips about blacks who emulate whites and he had hated everything about this singer. When he calmed down enough to tell me who he was slanging it turned out to be Lovelace Watkins. I can only think Lovelace's streaky grey hair must have looked blond on Yaphet's black and white television set.

Lovelace has been a friend of mine since Luisa and I met him in the Bahamas and I was as much amused as miffed with Yaphet for leading off about him that way so I invented the 'Lovelace Watkins running gag'. The first thing I did was to send Yaphet a telegram which read:

'Hear you have been saying nice things about me stop I would love to come and lunch stop arriving one today.' It was signed Lovelace Watkins. Next he had a phone call from Earl Jolly Brown posing as Lovelace and then I picked up a glossy publicity still of the singer from ATV offices and sent it to Yaphet inscribed: 'Kindest regards Lovelace Watkins.' Vic Heutschy, the American publicist, had a stroke of genius in Harrods and bought a poster which anyone can have made up with whatever they choose. Vic had 'Bond is Back! Lovelace Watkins and Roger Moore star in Live and Let Die.' 'Crackers' had Lovelace Watkins put on the call sheet as dialogue coach and today we decided that when we come to the scene where I have to drown Yaphet in a pool we will put Lovelace on the call sheet as swimming coach. Yaphet is going absolutely mad because he is uncertain how much is fact and how much is fiction. I thought of calling Lovelace for lunch at the studio if he is working in the London area but someone said it might be a bad idea. Indeed, I shouldn't like to cause a confrontation between him and Yaphet, for although Yaphet stands six foot three, Lovelace is about his match in height, heavier and a former heavyweight boxing champion.

We are looking forward to lunch on Sunday with Guy

and Kerima and Bryan Forbes and his wife, Nanette Newman. Bryan and I were in the same army unit when I was a captain and he was a sergeant. Years later the tables were turned and he became my boss at EMI-MGM when he was head of the studio and I was making *The Man Who Haunted Himself* there. We are planning a film together in the not too distant future. I have written the story, Bryan will write the screenplay and produce and I will direct but I won't appear in it.

The indoor swimming pool at our house had sand on the bottom and as I swam through the water I could see winged beetles swimming alongside me and large frogs sitting motionless on the bottom. It was then I noticed the turtles and I pointed them out to Luisa who came through the glass doors to the pool area just as a large fish floated through the air. Out of the corner of my eye I glimpsed a ten foot alligator and I shouted: 'Out! Luisa! Out!' We both fled and the alarm went off and it was six o'clock and time to get up for B-Day Sixty-one.

We started work today on Pinewood's lofty D stage where for the past weeks carpenters and plasterers have been at work building Mr Big's underground workshop. Dominating the subterranean cavern, where monorails disappear down tunnels and overhead carrying rails criss-cross like a crazy meccano set, is a huge lake where Mr Big will meet his end at the hands of Bond. It is the biggest set I have ever worked on and when I visited it last night to see where I would be working today it looked in the mysterious and gloomy half-light like some giant Aladdin's cave. No wonder I dreamed strange dreams!

After Bond saves Solitaire from sacrifice at Baron Samedi's black magic ceremony (yet to be shot) and escapes with her into the underground caves they are captured by Mr Big and imprisoned in his workshop. We filmed part of the cave scene in Jamaica in real underground caves and there is only one thing missing from our carpenter's cavernous reconstruction at Pinewood: the bats, thank goodness.

These big sets are time consumers because every time the camera moves the whole thing has to be re-lit and Jane and I are going to spend several hours strung together high up on the meccano set construction before the scene is in the can. It is pretty warm at our level but sparks stuck high in the gantry with the glittering brutes say it is hot as hell up there. I can't say I was sorry to get home tonight and when Luisa asked me how the day went I couldn't resist saying: 'Oh, we were just hanging around most of the day.'

This evening I chaired my first meeting of the Stars Organization for Spastics at the Regents Park headquarters and suffered badly from first night nerves in front of such SOS stalwarts as Sylvia Syms, Leslie Crowther and David Jacobs. Our President, the Hon Mrs James Ogilvy, introduced me and the first item on the agenda that I had to read was that Sir Charles Clore was chairman of the Joan Sutherland concert. It came out as Sir Charles Chairman is cloreman of—Mumbled minutes later I managed to get it right and perhaps I'll improve with practice.

The meeting lasted an hour and a half and I got back home to Denham tired out after a pretty arduous day. So much for the glamorous life a film star leads. No sumptuous supper of caviar by candlelight, Luisa brought me bacon and eggs in bed.

B-Day Sixty-two and a calypso 'Belly to Belly Back to Back' which haunted us in Jamaica ran through my head all day. That was because Jane and I spent the day roped together standing upright on a movable platform suspended from the top of the giant meccano set twenty feet above the underground lake as Mr Big's prisoners. Jane, lashed by her wrists around my waist, is terrified of heights and shook like a leaf.

It was not an easy day. I loathe bad feeling on the set and find it very difficult to work when there is tension. Guy, who is one of the nicest people around and a talented, well-organized director, has a problem with Yaphet, which seems to stem from the way Yaphet sees his role and Guy's differing interpretation of it. I go along with Guy, perhaps because I am green with envy at Yaphet's villainous role. Having played heroes for so many years I would love to get my teeth into a real baddy role, especially in a Bond film where they are larger than life and have all the best lines.

David Hedison is back with us, this time with his wife, Bridget, and they spent the weekend at our house. Joan Collins and her husband, Ron Kass, was there with her sister, Jackie Collins with her husband Oscar Lerman. Jackie penned the best selling books *The World is Full of Married Men* and *The Stud*. Luisa tried her hand at cooking a chicken curry and not to be outdone I made it a joint effort with a beef curry. We thoroughly enjoyed ourselves in the kitchen juggling chutney, mango, desiccated coconut and grated walnuts. It was voted a culinary delight by our guests who I had wisely primed with PV before dinner. PV is pink vodka, a new drink of my own invention which requires ice cold vodka poured over six drops of angostura bitters, whirled in a wine glass and tossed back in a gulp. In actual fact it tastes like medicine but, being a hypochondriac from way back, I find it appeals to my taste!

B-Day Sixty-three; still swinging roped together over the pool, Jane still shaking even though it is our third day strung up in the rafters. She recently revealed to the *News of the World*'s Weston Taylor that she was a virgin until the day she married and to keep her mind off the vertigo I teased her about it mercilessly. I think it helped; she was too busy trying to kick me to think about the twenty feet drop.

Today I made my escape with the aid of 007's magic watch which is equipped with a hyper-intensified magnetic field to attract metal objects. Bond uses it to arm himself with a gas pellet which Mr Big has taken from him and left lying on a table. The pellet with a puncture pin attached is for a shark gun and when fired into a shark inflates it to barrage balloon-like proportions. The pellet flies through the air and attaches itself to Bond's watch with a click. Next, with his hands tied behind his back, he manages to activate the saw-edged ring which circles his watch face to cut his ropes.

Not only back to back today but back to front because we shot a sequence which takes place before Bond and Solitaire are lifted aloft. We are trussed together on the platform before being hoisted high over the water while Mr Big, smiling sadistically, slides back my sweater sleeves and slices several fine cuts on my forearm. Cinema-goers will see blood begin to trickle from Mr Big's delicately drawn cuts. The cutting shot is a close-up. Off camera a tube, which fed flowing 'blood' to the blade, was attached to the knife handle.

It becomes clear why Mr Big has cut Bond as Whisper winches the pinioned pair over the water. An iron grid-like gate separates the underground pool from the sea. It opens and fast moving sharks' fins scythe through the surface, tanta-lized by the trickle of blood from Bond's arm. As Bond and Solitaire are being lowered into the sharks' fin soup Jimmy, free from his ropes, swings from the platform booting Whisper backwards into one of the torpedo-type containers used to transport heroin underwater. Mr Big's manic laughter stops abruptly when the canister clangs shut on Whisper; he pulls a knife and advances on Bond. But that is another B-Day.

*　　*　　*

B-Day Sixty-four was the day Bond got to grips with Mr Big. Geoffrey Holder, our Baron Samedi, choreographed the knife fight and proved himself as adept at the deadly as he is at the dance. He brought a fresh flair to the fight formula with what he calls his 'cobra stance'; a hypnotic and graceful death dance performed by Yaphet, who came up with a couple of slick suggestions of his own which he must have learned in Harlem. He gave them to me to use and they make a good fight finish. It was to have ended with Mr Big teetering on the edge of the pool before slapping back into the water but now I disarm him with a couple of sharp kicks and a karate chop; he grabs me by the throat, we both fall struggling into the water and I pop the gas pellet in his mouth which explodes ballooning Mr Big to a colossal caricature. Yaphet says he cannot swim so we are having to use a double for some of the shots. I do the whole sequence with the gas pellet like some great gum boil in my mouth ready to thrust it down Mr Big's throat and my face felt stiff at the end of the day.

Last night Kirk and Anne Douglas gave a splendid farewell dinner party for friends in England before leaving for their Hollywood home. At dinner I talked to the Duke of Bedford's beautiful daughter-in-law, Lady Tavistock, who as Henrietta Tiarks was Deb of her year, and who used to be President of the Stars Organization for Spastics, so naturally our talk turned to the Charity.

We are having dramas with the *Live and Let Die* première date because the Duke of Edinburgh won't be available on 12 July, nor will Princess Anne, or Prince Charles who is at sea for six months with the Royal Navy. It looks like the date will have to be changed.

B-Day Sixty-five. I was tanked up today in more ways than one. After four soaking wet hours grappling with Mr Big in the water tank I broke my golden rule and got tanked in the studio bar, wending my way home two hours and several stiff scotches later when my circulation had returned to something like normal.

I managed to sandwich between shivering shots an interview with a lady writer from *Woman* whose questions had centred on Roger Moore, the family man. I discussed my aversion to hanging around pubs after shooting and said I preferred to be home and have a spell with the children before bedtime. In all the years I have worked at Pinewood I don't think I have been in the bar more than a couple of times and never at night. Tonight as I downed my warming whiskies and the evening was beginning to get a glow on who should walk into the bar but the lady journalist. If I had been sober I would have had the grace to look shamefaced but instead I let out a cheery hello, smartly followed by a loud hiccough. It was too late to tell her that Luisa was spending the week in Rome with her family and the children were staying with friends.

The extra time in the tank was my own fault because when I saw rushes of what we shot yesterday I discovered my teeth were clamped so tightly over the gas pellet that not only had I pulled the most extraordinary faces but I looked toothless to boot. Guy agreed in spite of the great expense to restage part of the fight scene.

But it was not quite the same scene as yesterday. This time Yaphet spurned the use of a double and went in the water himself. We had all believed him when he said he couldn't swim, especially as he added: 'Where could a kid in Harlem learn to swim?' But swim he certainly can.

It is an impossible task to keep the static tank water clean and despite regular skimmings, dust, dirt and paint drippings had settled on the surface and the tons of chlorine added for cleanliness created havoc with my sore, red-rimmed eyes. The water is supposed to be kept at a steady warm temperature but today it was mysteriously icy and I think I know why. I beat Harry at cards on Sunday and he couldn't afford to pay the heating bill.

One side of the oblong tank is transparent so the camera can show the underwater action and I got out hastily between takes because apart from the cold I was beginning to feel like a goldfish. After complaining at rehearsals the water was too cold and refusing to stay in, Yaphet then went in and refused to come out, deciding to dress in the water. He insisted on struggling into his light silk suit, shirt and shoes while splashing about in the tank. It took him fifteen minutes to get into costume and Guy was so brassed off with it all that he walked off the set and wouldn't come back until he, Guy, was ready to shoot.

Yaphet mutters things like: 'Listen, man, I have two friends who died because things weren't worked out and I'm worried about acting, man.' We also had trouble with the large pockets on his silk suit. They filled up with air and he couldn't stay submerged so he was weighted down with a lead-loaded belt around his waist. He found he could not surface and he hurriedly discarded it.

I am still besieged by journalists as I was in New Orleans and Jamaica. They don't come in ones and twos any more, they come in teams. Today a television team from Holland clambered all over the set asking how my Bond will be any different from Sean's in Dutch. Next week a Japanese team is coming. I wonder how the question sounds in Japanese.

B-Day Sixty-six and I have just spent a romantic weekend in Paris with Luisa; she flying from Rome and me from London after an early wrap on Friday. We enjoyed a splendid dinner at a little Parisian haunt of ours round the corner from the Hotel Georges V, or the George Sank as the Americans call it. The week-end wasn't all pleasure. Harry asked me if I would visit the Crazy Horse and look the girls over for a likely lass to play a scene in the picture which calls for a busty beauty. Ever devoted to duty I stoically sat through two hours striptease and Luisa very kindly came along, too. I passed my opinion to Harry and told him if *really* necessary I would go back and have another look with him. Oh, the burdens of Bond! In Paris we saw the controversial *Last Tango in Paris* which is not showing in England yet. My verdict: a blue movie starring Marlon Brando.

David Hedison and I spent today in another night club; or rather James Bond and Felix Leiter did. We shot the beginning of the sequence which ends with 007 sinking through the floor and landing at Mr Big's feet in his Fillet of Soul hideout. My part called for little more than a request to a waiter for the familiar Martini, shaken not stirred, but I am interrupted by Felix who asks: 'Where's your sense of adventure?' and insists on ordering mint juleps as this is New Orleans. Unlike the New York Fillet of Soul restaurant this one has a band and a singer, Sister Love, played by Brenda Arnau who was such a success on the London stage in *Oh! Calcutta!* She sings the theme song *Live and Let Die* as Bond's table disappears and Felix Leiter returns from a decoy telephone call to find two mint juleps and an empty chair at a substitute table a waiter whips into place.

Paul McCartney has written the song and I had lunch today with the man who is arranging the music, George Martin, who was responsible for so many of the Beatles' hits. It is a tremendous piece of music and I will stick my neck out and say that three weeks from its release it will be number one in the charts. It's not last year's music, it's not even this year's music, it's next year's.

Luisa and I are off to the opening of Rags tonight; a new restaurant owned by friends of ours, Johnny Gold and Oscos Lerman. It doesn't officially open until tomorrow so I suppose you could call tonight a dress rehearsal.

*   *   *

B-Day Sixty-seven was a black day for me because I learned of the deaths of two good friends. In the morning I was in the middle of an interview with a journalist from *Good Housekeeping* when I was asked to take a call from *Reveille* because they were doing a tribute to Maurice Woodruff and wanted a quote from me. The word 'tribute' should have warned me but I took the call and a voice said: 'We are talking to people who knew Maurice Woodruff—'

'Who knew,' I interrupted, 'you make it sound as though he were dead.'

'He is,' said the voice, and went on to tell me that Maurice had died the day before of a heart attack in Singapore. I was shaken and numbed by the news because I had known Maurice for seventeen years. He had made many predictions for me and all of them true. How I hate Singapore. It was there a couple of years ago that Luisa and I picked up a paper and read of the death of another dear friend, Hollywood actor, Jeff Hunter, whom my son Geoffrey is named after. Singapore now has two marks against for me and I am not looking forward to going there in the autumn for *Man with the Golden Gun.*

I got home tonight to a phone call from Stephen Gilbert telling me his father, actor Henry Gilbert, had died. Henry worked with me on the Saint series and accompanied Luisa and me on a trip to Israel last year. It was particularly distressing to hear of both deaths in one day.

B-Day Sixty-eight was voodoo day for Bond. Solitaire, who lost more than her occult powers after a night of love with Bond, is to be sacrificed at a voodoo rite on the island of San Monique presided over by Baron Samedi. No longer a virgin, her tell-tale powers have terminated and Mr Big, betrayed and incensed, has decreed her death.

The Art Department built a very convincing pile of huge plaster rocks on scaffolding where Bond hides to watch the voodoo worshippers gather. The General ordered me up to the top of this vast pile from where I was to make my cautious descent to rescue Solitaire. I began gingerly to pick my way over the plaster, mindful of the last time I was on a 'mountain' set. It was a snow-covered scene on a stage at Warner Brothers Studio in Hollywood and obeying the director's shouted command I clambered over a high rock and disappeared right through the plaster. A piece of tubular scaffolding which I straddled saved me from a sixty feet fall to the ground below. Hats off to the Pinewood construction team. Their 'rocks' felt more solid than Mount Snowdon.

After creeping down the rocks Bond hides behind one of the gravestones and sees Solitaire in a ragged white 'Cinderella' dress dragged over to two stakes and roped between them. A coffin is carried on, the lid opened and a sinister gentleman wearing an ass's head reaches inside and brings out a seven foot long snake which he raises above his head to the screams of the crowd as he begins a wild dance in front of Solitaire.

Plucky Jane never flinched although she must have been pretty scared as this very active, lethal-looking reptile was waved in front of her face. The voodoo sacrifice is a speciality Mr Big reserves for certain victims. One is CIA agent, Baines, who stumbles on Mr Big's secret before Bond and dies for it. Dennis Edwards, who plays Baines, was strung between the same two posts two days ago. He spent several hours eyeball to eyeball with the writhing snake while in the background the voodoo drums throbbed and four dozen dancers swayed and chanted. Suddenly the snake's head darted and its scaly skin skimmed Dennis's neck. It was seconds before the crowd on the set realized he had blacked out because he was held upright by his bonds.

The repelling job of holding our coiling co-star goes to Michael Ebbin who plays the High Priest wearing little more than the asses head. Yesterday, Michael, who miraculously manages to keep the snake's head aimed away from him while he does his High Priest's dance, came unstuck. The snake's head spun and it sank its fangs in his forearm. Production stopped while one of its teeth was pulled from a puncture in Michael's arm and replaced with a hypodermic syringe of anti-poison serum. Not surprisingly it took time to persuade Michael that he must resume his acquaintanceship with his wriggling rival and complete the scene.

All this must have been in Jane's mind as the dancers began to weave around her, the snake held aloft and spitting venom over her heaving bosom. The High Priest's dance suddenly stops and all eyes turn to the graveyard where a grey topper sprinkled with blood and sprouting chicken feathers lies on a tomb. As they watch, the topper rises in the air and out of the black of the grave the weird figure of Baron Samedi emerges, his body painted like a skeleton and his head like a skull. The High Priest lets out a short high-pitched scream, tom-toms begin again. This is the signal for the filthy serpent to ravage Solitaire's lovely neck. In the nick of time Jim draws his Smith and Wesson .44 chromium plated Magnum and fires at the High Priest; swivels to Samedi firing straight at his head and body. Samedi's figure shatters and before the horror-stricken crowd realize it is only a dummy, 007 leaps over the wall to free Solitaire. When we did that bit I was better on the take than in rehearsal when I managed to spread-eagle myself across the wall and skin both my shins. All in all it was quite a hectic day for Jimmy Bond.

The Japanese invaded Pinewood today waving movie cameras, notebooks, tape recorders and their interpreter. At the end of a long and difficult interview for television, where everything the interviewer asked in Japanese had to be translated into English and my subsequent reply translated into Japanese, they asked me to send the viewers a message in their own language. I foolishly agreed thinking it would be something simple like 'sayonara' when they presented me with a seemingly endless scroll which must have been my life story in Japanese. I chickened out; it would have taken me a life time of linguaphone to learn to pronounce it.

The German magazine *Stern* also sent a reporter (Ve haf vays of making you give an interview). *Stern* is responsible for the current drama involving the real-life 'M' whose son figured in a drugs case. *Stern* decided to reveal M's identity in defiance of a British Government 'D' Notice which forbade publication under the Official Secrets Act. English newspapers which had the identification observed the 'D' Notice then felt as *Stern* had broken the ban they might as well publish, too. Today there were frenzied phone calls to and from my dressing room where the *Stern* reporter was interviewing me and his West German headquarters. Another writer here today was Norma Shearer's nephew, Lloyd Shearer, whose father, Douglas Shearer, I knew when he was an MGM executive.

I am still trying to sort out the première for the Stars Organization for Spastics and the latest edict from the Palace is that if one member of the Royal Family is in attendance there can be no other member present. Princess Anne is coming but the date is now 5 July, and Harry says we'll be lucky to get a dry print by then, meaning that the laboratory will barely have finished working on the strips of celluloid which are *Live and Let Die*.

I am scribbling my way through begging letters on behalf of the Joan Sutherland Concert in aid of the Stars Organization for Spastics. The response to an ordinary, rather formal request to buy tickets or advertising space in the brochure has amazed me. Sums from £5 to £100 come tumbling through the letter box by return post from people who are not even coming to the concert. I have been really touched by people's reaction.

* * *

B-Day Sixty-nine had its ups and downs; literally, because Bond and Solitaire escape from the voodoo ceremony by lift. A winch worked by Mr Big's henchman operates the lift which goes up and down between the underground caves and a grave in the voodoo cemetery. A few sharp taps on the tombstone with a machete by Bond and the grave opens up revealing the lift. Bond and Solitaire are carried down to the caves where 007 dispatches Mr Big's astonished liftman with a swift kick in the mouth and summarily scatters several others who rush him. Grabbing Solitaire by the hand he hares through steel doors set in the rock.

Jane and I spent most of the day standing on a platform, twenty to thirty feet above ground making our jerky descent. Poor Jane with her aversion to heights was petrified. She has gone through a lot these last few weeks, more than most people are asked to face in a lifetime and she has taken it like a trooper, or paratrooper, if you'll forgive the pun. She clung nervously to my arm as I wisecracked about the drop to distract her. The words were barely out when the lift plummeted six or eight feet. Jane fell in a heap and as she tumbled to the edge I grabbed the only part of her I could reach; her waist long hair. I got a good grip on it and tugged. She yelled with fright and surprise. Below a white and shaking crew man explained that the ratchet on the hydraulic lift had broken.

My stomach didn't take too kindly to being lifted up and down all day after a welcome home party for Michael Caine and his new bride, Shakira, just back from America. We were eighteen and guests included Peter Sellers, Joan Collins and Ron Cass, Jackie and Harry Saltzman and Michael Caine's daughter, Dominique, just returned from a Jamaican holiday. She stayed at the Half Moon Hotel and visited the crocodile farm where our sets are still standing.

Early in the evening David Picker, United Artist's top executive and Dan Rissner, the UK chief, came by and were very complimentary about an hour or so of the *Live and Let Die* footage they had seen. All sorts of predictions were being made, such as we would gross sixty million dollars first time out and England would make a million and a half pounds. I was very lucky to come through the evening without getting a bigger head than I've got already!

Talking of predictions I was happy to see all of mine come true on the Academy Award nominations. I guessed rightly that the line-up for best actor would be Michael Caine, Olivier, Peter O'Toole, Paul Winfield and Marlon Brando.

We are busy making plans for a holiday when the film is over. Luisa and I will fly from New York down to Acapulco where Leslie Bricusse has a house. Joan Collins will join us from London bringing both her children and ours.

Today Luisa threw a shower for Shakira. Twenty lovely ladies at the house, all without their husbands and me locked up in the studio. Marvellous, isn't it? My wife's not daft.

B-Day Seventy was a Royal Command Performance. Princess Alexandra, the Hon Angus Ogilvy and their eight-year-old son, James, who had asked to see 007 in action, paid a visit to the set and watched me do my stuff as Bond. I offered to show James my Smith and Wesson and told him it was among the most powerful guns in the world. He touched it very gingerly as if terrified it might go off in his face. I told him if anyone got bumped off around the studio this afternoon I now had his finger prints on the butt.

I am always amazed at the memories of the Royal Family. I introduced Luisa to Princess Alexandra who said: 'Oh, yes. I haven't seen you since the World Wildlife Party at the Talk of the Town.' Pity she remembered really since Luisa was standing there today in a full length mink coat. The Hon James Ogilvy, Angus's brother, whose wife, June, is the

Stars Organization for Spastics President, has the city office where Ian Fleming once worked and has invited me along to lunch one day to see it. His wife telephoned me last night with the bad news that I will present the line-up of guests to the Duchess of Kent at the Joan Sutherland concert and I am dreading it. Nadia Nerina, the ballerina, is throwing a party after the concert at which Joan Sutherland with receive a memento of the evening and I will have to make the presentation speech. I get neurotic about making speeches and I have let myself in for another one on Saturday when I am guest of honour at the British Kinematograph Society dinner at the Savoy. Graham Stark, who I tapped for speech ideas, has telephoned Benny Hill, Frankie Howerd and practically every comedian in the country collecting jokes for me but even with illustrious script writers like those I am still nervous. I dislike after-dinner speaking. It's not the same as appearing before a camera with a prepared script: I am sure everyone is bored to death and all my jokes are laying eggs. One of the funniest lines I heard last night at the Variety Club dinner where some of the country's quickest wits gather came, not in a speech but from Mike Caine's wife, Shakira. Formerly, Shakira Baksh and 'Miss Guyana', she told us that a US newspaper had mis-spelt her name as Shakira Backlash.

One of the numerous nice things about the Variety Club dinner was the kippers and pots of tea served at one o'clock in the morning. A perfect way to round off an evening.

B-Day Seventy-one. Out of voodoo land and into a railway carriage where Bond and Solitaire are on their way from New Orleans to New York after disposing of Mr Big. The scene brought back memories of the New Orleans railway station where we shot the exterior of the scene. Homesick and hungover that morning I recall how fervently I wished it was Paddington Station with my home only half an hour's drive away.

Mr Big is now dead but his right hand man, Tee Hee, bent on revenge has tracked Bond and Solitaire to the train. Julius and I have been rehearsing our fight scene for the past few days and we are both tired out. The leg I injured in New Orleans has been playing up and I have been having short wave therapy and manipulation treatment but I was such a wreck last night I was too tired to haul myself to hospital.

The railway carriage where our fight takes place is built on a shoulder-high platform and we must have climbed up and down as frequently today as a footplate man does in a fortnight. A former Festival ballet dancer, Jane, foolishly and flippantly claimed she could stretch her legs wider than mine and I couldn't resist the riposte: 'I didn't have to do that to get in pictures, duckie.'

Jane had a trying day being dragged around by me and then she tripped and twisted her knee; part of the platform collapsed with her on it and by the time we were ready to wrap her eyes were red and puffy and whenever I spoke to her she burst into tears. A large brandy pepped her up and put the pink back in her cheeks.

The *Daily Express* published pictures of yesterday's Royal visit showing young James standing between me and his father and gazing up in wide-eyed wonderment at me in my 007 gear. The headline, I felt, was rather unfortunate. 'Why can't you be like him Daddy?' it asked. I whipped off a telegram to the Hon Angus Ogilvy. It read: 'It was not my headline and apart from that my son wants to know why I am not like you.'

B-Day Seventy-two and we are still speeding through the night on the darkened train to New York. James Bond is attacked by Tee Hee who mysteriously appears from inside a

162

mail sack in the luggage compartment, cutting his way out of the bag with his claw. In Bond's sleeping berth he clips through the metal chain suspending Solitaire's bunk to the wall and it swings up shutting her inside, which was not the kind of bunk-up she had in mind. Then Tee Hee takes on Bond. Bond rips Tee Hee's jacket sleeve exposing the intricate system of pulley wires which work his artificial arm. As Bond is slammed back against the train window he grabs Solitaire's scissors and cuts the central wire pulley in the arm completely disabling Tee Hee before heaving him through the window as the train thunders across a canyon.

Julius and I had been knocking hell out of each other all morning and were more than ready for a little light relief which came in the shops of some B for bosoms. The search I started in Paris for another Bond bird was still on. She appears in the opening sequence of the film and is supposed to be Italian, dark haired and lusciously built. None of the girls seen had appealed to Harry, Cubby, Guy, or even myself. Not that my casting vote is that important, but I thought it was my turn to make a few suggestions.

My nominees, Madeline Smith and Vivian Neaves were brought down today to meet Guy and Harry. Both girls worked with me on *The Persuaders!* Vivian Neaves is famous for being the first nude to appear in an advertisement in *The Times*. She arrived in a blue Levi outfit and a suntan from a recent photo session in Israel. It was cold and the buttons of her denim jacket were done up to the neck where they were feeling the strain. Come to that, so were the crew! They had just recovered from Vivian's impact when Madeline walked in. The choice between such equally beautiful girls could not have been easy but Madeline ended up a few inches ahead.

As production comes to a close pressure mounts with last minute interviews and last minute stills sessions; each more important than the last and each with a twenty-four hour deadline. I dare not complain or they will point out that my son gets more publicity than me. Several pictures of him were taken with the lovely Julie Ege's daughter at a party recently of which one appeared in the *Sunday Mirror*. He took the glare of publicity quite calmly, merely asking: 'Where's the other photographs they took of me?'

B-Day Seventy-three. This afternoon saw the end of the longest train journey of my life. It was a sad journey's end because I said goodbye to Jane and Julius. On the tag line of the day and her very last line in *Live and Let Die* Jane burst into tears. I told her when she had been in the business as long as her Uncle Roger these things would pass without emotion. Although it is always sad when a film is finished the feeling passes pretty quickly. She said at sixteen when her first professional job in pantomime was over she cried for two days. I've known actors cry when a film is finished because it means they are out of work and sometimes, particularly in European productions, because they haven't been paid. It doesn't happen in England and America but it is not uncommon on the Continent. I was making a picture which shall be nameless in Italy and discovered from my agents that I was not being paid. I took it up with the producer who pleaded that he intended to pay.

'Intending and paying are two different things,' I told him hotly.

'I am sure he *will* pay,' Luisa soothed.

'I'm sure he will too, because I'll belt him if he doesn't,' I told her.

I decided that a bandaged producer would not help my bank balance and evolved a better way to handle it. I checked my pay every Friday and if it was missing so was I the following Monday. It worked every time.

Saying goodbye to fellow actors is always a sad moment. If I had to pick a favourite on this picture it would be Julius Harris, both as a marvellous human being and as a brilliant character actor. When I do a scene with him and see the rushes I find it hard to believe that this evil, vicious character with rolling eyes and maniacal titter is really our gentle Julius. Our scenes in the train together were tough but he never lost his humour. We were lucky to escape with just bruises and not cuts because the plate glass of the train window was broken at least six times. Each time we broke it 'Crackers' suggested Perspex was used and each time it was replaced with sheet glass. Tee Hee's metal arm caused problems because as Julius and I threw ourselves round the confined space of the carriage in what could have been a perfect take the mechanism would go wrong and we would have to begin again. I took a couple of whacks on the jaw and kicks in the gut during our fight but I don't think I came out of it as badly as Julius who really took a hammering because, after all, Bond has to win.

When shooting ended this afternoon it wasn't the end of the working day for me. I spent another hour and a half in the post synching theatre linking my voice to the picture on the screen. When shooting on location the sound recording quality is often poor, through no fault of the sound crew but because background noises sometimes dominate instead of the actors' voices. Some actors find it hard but I do not have much difficulty. The trick is to keep in mind the thought you had when you said the line originally and not only will it recur exactly the same but you can even improve on the original. Come to think of it I've seen some of my pictures dubbed by other actors into foreign languages and I have been greatly improved by the translation.

I got home tonight to be met by a remorseful Luisa whose fractured English had finally let her down and resulted in Mrs Cubby Broccoli whiling away a fruitless hour at the White Elephant waiting for Luisa to turn up for lunch. At 2 o'clock she telephoned Luisa at home and thinking she must have mistaken the day asked were they supposed to have lunched today, Tuesday, or not.

'Yes, darlink, on Tersday,' replied Luisa happily.

'Yes, Tuesday,' said puzzled Mrs Broccoli.

'That's right,' said Luisa. 'Tersday. The day after Wednesday.'

To Luisa's Italian ear there is no difference between Tuesday and Thursday and it has cost me a large bouquet of flowers.

'Charming,' I told her. 'You don't turn up and I pay for the flowers.'

B-Day Seventy-four was Bond By Appointment Day. HRH Prince Mohammed of Jordan, King Hussein's brother, came to lunch at Pinewood and saw me in action as Bond. He came with six personal bodyguards, two Special Branch men and Tessa Kennedy, whose flair for interior décor enhanced Hussein's palace in Jordan. Four further bodyguards had been left behind in London. I had forgotten that I had agreed to have lunch with Don Forbes from the Associated Press News Agency and as they are choosy about who they talk to and the interview had taken a lot of setting up I could hardly cancel it, so Don was invited to join our table. What with the bodyguards, the Special Branch men, the Press and the Prince we were a large luncheon party and Luisa, who was lunching with Viviane Ventura and John Bentley's mother with his two children, had to take a separate table.

After lunch Guy screened the boat chase sequence for the Prince's party and they seemed delighted. They laughed and cheered in the right places although it surprises me that the screen exploits of James Bond seem so novel to Prince Mohammed, who is himself a black belt karate and judo expert. Back on set we chatted about guns and I asked him if he would like to see my Smith and Wesson ·44 magnum. I drew it but before eight bodyguards moved I hastily explained: 'It's not loaded, fellows,' hoping they would

166

believe me. It is easy to understand their unease. There have been attempts on his brother's life and at the youthful age of sixteen, he was with his grandfather when he was assassinated. It is only days since the Israelis shot down the Libyan airliner so their anxiety is intensified.

I told the Prince that, before playing Bond, I was in the White Elephant one day for lunch. Sitting at a table to my right was Sean Connery and to my left Moshe Dayan with several bodyguards. The head waiter came over and whispered in my ear:

'What does he want with all those bodyguards when he's got 007 and The Saint?'

After the royal party left, David Hedison, Roy Stewart and I got down to the business in hand, which was front projection. This is an extraordinary process which will look on screen as though we are bouncing about in a boat on the open sea but in fact the boat is on dry studio land: a film of the open sea is projected on to a screen behind us giving the impression that we are on the water.

Shooting ended and I rushed home to change and get to London to keep my second Royal appointment, this time with HRH The Duchess of Kent at the Joan Sutherland concert in aid of the Stars Organization for Spastics. We just made the Albert Hall in time, driving through London's sole snow storm this winter. It was 7.10 when we arrived and there was barely time to make sure I knew the names of the people lined up for me to present to Her Royal Highness. When the Duchess arrived I started off quite confidently down the line presenting Sir Charles Clore, Mr and Mrs Leslie Grade, Mr and Mrs David Land—and then, glancing over my right shoulder at the next in line to be presented, I saw a face I just couldn't put a name to. My heart sank while I searched my mind desperately and it came to me in the nick of time. Of all people to forget it was Nadia Nerina's husband, Charles Gordon, and they were throwing the party for Joan Sutherland after the concert. Nearly a number one gaff but in my defence I had only met him once before.

Escorting the Duchess of Kent into the Royal Box was sort of scary. In my apprehension I recalled the typed instructions I had received. They said: 'You will sit on the Duchess's right hand,' and I remember thinking 'How uncomfortable. I am sure she would rather I sat on a chair.'

It was a superb concert and even my speech of thanks to everybody at the party afterwards went well: much to my relief, and best of all, we made £15,000 for the spastics.

Madeline Smith was in the studio today being photographed in a fetching negligee. I called 'Goodnight, darling,' to her as I rushed off for the concert and she called back:

'I'll see you in bed tomorrow,' which is one way of saying goodnight.

B-Day Seventy-five was the day I bedded my third Bond bird; a lovely Italian secret agent played by voluptuous Madeline Smith. In the script it is the first scene of the picture and on screen she is the first girl I kiss in my new role as Bond, but the shooting sequence had me turning my attentions to Gloria, then Jane, before splitting the sheets with the magnificent Madeline.

Our pillow appointment was in a broad bed in Bond's London mews flat, an elegantly furnished construction on 'B' stage. A production point which seems to strike first-time visitors to a film studio is that sets built for interior shots rarely have roofs, so that light can blaze in from above. We began early; as Bond's flat was roofless Madeline and myself were exposed to the draughts which whistled round the stage and the bed was icy.

Props had not provided hot water bottles, no doubt taking the view that anyone in bed with Madeline would find them superfluous. They forgot that the first shot called for me, slumbering soundly, to bounce Madeline's head off my chest and bound out of bed when the doorbell rang and there was an alarming banging of knockers, if you'll pardon yet another pun.

All this did not work in one take and, what with rehearsals and slip-ups, I bounded and rebounded in and out of bed all morning, my feet freezing with every leap. It would have tarnished Bond's image to have worn woolly socks and I envied Madeline who, although bare from the waist up, could slide under the bed clothes; she squealed every time my cold feet made contact with her knees.

Awakened by the banging on the front door, Bond looks at his watch and finds that it is 5.45 in the morning. Being Bond's watch, it is no ordinary timepiece but a wrist computer: if you press a button, red neon digital figures light up on the blank black face. It is the world's most perfect timepiece.

Only one person would dare to wake Bond at that time; his secret service boss, M. For Bond, it might be no great pleasure to see M, but for me it was splendid to see Bernard Lee in M's mantle. Weeks ago I was told that Bernard was not well, but he certainly seems his fit, friendly self now. He is an old mate and it is nice to work with him again.

With M, who orders Bond to investigate the sudden disappearance of agents who were probing Mr Big's insidious business, is Miss Moneypenny – played by another mate, in fact a former class-mate, Lois Maxwell. We were in the same year at the Royal Academy of Dramatic Art. As M might discover the presence of the svelte *signorina* who is absent from the Italian Secret Service, Bond invites him in with trepidation. To his relief the naked girl has disappeared, but has unfortunately hidden herself in the wardrobe where Bond hangs M's coat. The situation is saved by the knowing Miss Moneypenny, who extracts the coat without revealing the denuded agent.

M leaves and, sighing with relief, Bond lets the *signorina,* who has now donned her dress, out of the wardrobe. He has a couple of hours to spare before catching his trans-atlantic plane, and does not intend to waste them.

As if a computer watch were not enough, Miss Money-penny has delivered Bond's intriguing magnetic timepiece. He embraces the *signorina*, then, holding the watch magnet near the long back zip on her dress, delicately draws his wrist down the line of her spine without touching her. The metal zip responds and the dress falls to the floor.

'What a gentle touch you have, James,' she whispers.

'Sheer magnetism,' I reply.

It may seem like money for jam pressed close to the beautiful Madeline Smith and taking her clothes off into the bargain, but on the twentieth take your arm is aching, you've got cramp in your left foot and your right knee is going to sleep. Part of the trouble was that Madeline's dress just would not fall far enough down; probably due to her self-supporting anatomy. Julie Harris, the costume designer, had to go down on her knees off camera and gently pull the dress down. As the watch is by no means magnetic Crackers was also down there on his knees with his hands up Madeline's skirt pulling a hidden wire attached to the end of the zip – so the floor around our feet was getting pretty crowded.

When I arrived home from the studio the children asked me, as they always do, 'What did you do today, Daddy?' I wasn't quite sure what to tell them. I could hardly say, 'I was in bed with a lady this morning and I made twenty attempts to take her dress off this afternoon.'

Tonight I announced one of the winners of the Society of Film and Television Arts awards at the Royal Albert Hall – Liza Minelli for her role in *Cabaret*. Luisa rushed me into my 'soup and fish' when I got home and we raced around to leave the house in plenty of time for the drive to London, because police warned that a one-day rail strike was causing huge traffic jams. I think they say this on purpose to keep the roads clear, because we got to London in record time and had to wait fifteen minutes for the Albert Hall to open.

Everyone involved in the show was liberally plied with drink backstage and the chattering throng included Oliver Reed, Hywel Bennett, Christopher Lee, Robert Vaughan, and Nina Baden-Semper. Sitting calmly watching the proceedings on a monitor, then drawling unmistakably, 'Very nice to meet you' when someone was introduced, was that Hollywood legend, James Stewart; that same look, that same voice, that same quiet, composed presence I have admired magnified on the movie screen for so long. What a pleasure to meet him.

B-Day Seventy-six, our last day of shooting at Pinewood Studios. When next I go before the cameras as Bond it will be in New York with a mostly American unit, so today was the last working day for almost all of our English crew.

I spent a good deal of the day strung up in my kite harness for a close-up of me swooping down on to the lawn of Solitaire's eyrie, which was not nearly so nerve-racking as the real thing had been in Jamaica. Dangling a few feet off the studio floor is certainly preferable to swinging in the air over needle-sharp rocks. I had to get back into the railway carriage, too, for a final shot of the fight scene with Tee Hee which Guy decided he wanted, but as Julius has left we used a double.

Still missing from Pinewood was the familiar face of Lana Turner. The film she was due to make there had been delayed and so, consequently, had her arrival.

We climaxed today's shooting with the traditional and popular end-of-film party. Everyone on the unit and some of the studio staff, who have been so helpful, were there. We crowded into the Green Room overlooking the Pinewood lawns. Drinks were dispensed by the deft hands of three Pinewood waitresses and we helped ourselves to the buffet; I made a short 'thank you' speech to the crew and everyone concerned.

Afterwards I dashed off to a S O S meeting where we discussed how successful the Joan Sutherland fund-raising concert had been, with a special vote of thanks going to Sir Charles Clore for the twelve thousand pounds in advertising revenue he had collected. He owns practically every shoe shop in Britain and I promised him I would always wear his shoes, although at the moment I am stepping into Sean Connery's. Talking of shoes, Bob Baker, the producer of *The Saint* and *The Persuaders!*, was with me in Rome when I decided I would treat myself to a pair of crocodile shoes from the most exclusive shoe shop on the Via Veneto. He offered to come with me and on the way over I regaled him with a discourse on how one must always buy from the skin of one reptile and not have shoes made up from bits and pieces. I was quite the expert on the dead crocodile in those days but had no idea how familiar I would one day become with live specimens. Carried away by my enthusiasm, Bob said he would have a pair too and if I would lend him the money he would pay me back at the hotel. Later he asked how much he owed me and I gave the price in lire.

'How much in pounds?' he asked.

'Forty,' I replied.

'Oh, for both pairs,' said Bob.

'No. Forty pounds *each*,' I stressed.

He went white and swore solemnly he would never, never wear them because he would be afraid of getting them dirty. I told Sir Charles Clore the story. 'Quite right,' said Sir Charles. 'I never spend more than four pounds on a pair of shoes.' It didn't occur to me at the time that he gets them from one of his own shops and as soon as they are dirty he throws them away.

* * *

A much depleted party boarded the Pan Am jumbo jet for New York compared with the *Live and Let Die* full team which had winged back from Jamaica in December. There was only Luisa, Guy, Crackers, Ted Moore, Harry and his secretary, Sue Parker, Elaine the Duchess and myself, from the Jamaica flight list. David Hedison completed our small party. One of the joys of jumbo travel is the first-class dining room; a welcome break from the old monotony of seven hours in a seat. At a table for four, and while Luisa, Guy and I tucked into caviare and Cornish game hen, Harry produced several plastic bags containing bagels, sour cream, smoked salmon and bananas. The bagels were quickly dispatched to the inflight kitchen to be heated up while he made inroads on the smoked salmon. Harry is wary of airline food; he doesn't suffer from mid-air malnutrition but always travels with his own in an assortment of bags.

After the meal we all made a serious effort to drain the plane dry. Guy and I were the only ones left on our feet by the end of the flight, although admittedly in a very mellow mood. The Bond magic got us through Customs without their opening every piece of luggage, as they so often do, and we were whisked off in limousines to our hotels; some to the Sherry-Netherland and the rest of us here to the Warwick.

New York, and I prowled around our apartment in the early morning dark looking for Cary Grant's old pretzels; I was so hungry I would have eaten anyone's old pretzels but the odds on finding my fellow Fabergé director's were better because Cary has lent Luisa and me his 27th-floor apartment in the Warwick Hotel while we are in New York.

Jet lag was upon me because our late-night arrival (London time) at Kennedy Airport was New York's early evening. We went straight to bed and I awoke fit but famished at four o'clock this morning with my stomach

173

telling me it was two hours past breakfast and no room service until 7 AM. All-night television is a boon to time travellers, and I sat bleary-eyed watching a 1935 Randolph Scott Western and drinking soda water until room service started and up came my bacon and eggs.

After breakfast I dozed again, to be jangled awake by the phone. It was Harry with his usual telephonic interrogative, 'What's new?' We exchanged 'What's new's' and 'nothings' and arranged to meet at what was once Fabergé's town house on 54th Street and is accommodating our production office while we are in New York. Harry suggested lunch at La Grotta Azzurra, so nine of us, including Cubby, Guy and Crackers, crushed into one car and breathed in all the way downtown to the Italian quarter and a stupendous meal. Stuffed mushrooms, baked clams, shrimp in garlic and tomato sauce, plates of pasta and my favourite dish, tripe Italian style. Cramming ourselves back into the car was even harder after lunch, especially as Harry, Cubby and Luisa had disappeared inside an Italian pastry shop and emerged clutching big bags full of giant cigar-shaped pastries filled with rich cream; they managed to nosh their way through them before arriving back at the hotel for large Alka-Seltzers and two hours shut-eye.

David Tebet, our friend at NBC, picked us up this evening and took us out to dinner. He said he knew just what we would enjoy: a little Italian food. He took us to Patsy's, Frank Sinatra's favourite Italian restaurant. Luisa and I waded through what we could but Harry didn't let the side down, topping it off with a large slab of rum cake crowned with a great blob of whipped cream.

Our hope that we would dodge the Press and curiosity calls about the forthcoming baby seems to have been fulfilled. Last week in London the word did leak and there were a few calls from Fleet Street. The day following our departure the *Sunday Express* printed two paragraphs, followed by a photograph of Luisa and me twenty-four

174

hours later in the *Daily Express*. With a bit of luck that will be that, and interest will have subsided by the time we return home.

B-Day Seventy-seven: Bond's first day in New York. We worked our way uptown to Harlem's 117th Street after some shots this morning midtown on 69th Street outside the mythical San Monique's Consulate, where Dr Kananga and Solitaire are seen arriving by Cadillac. Solitaire is seen but not Jane Seymour, who we have left in London. The New York scenes do not show Solitaire in close-up, so we are using a double; much to Jane's disappointment, as she has never seen New York.

Driving uptown to Harlem was an eerie experience. There is no welcome for whitey there; suspicion stalks the streets and, contrary to our usual experience, no crowd collects to stand and stare at the film crew at work. The streets look empty and forlorn, given over to grinding poverty, soaring crime and the deathly delusion of drugs.

Ted Moore and I shared a car to the location and as we drove across the dividing line of 110th Street into Harlem we stopped at a traffic light. The window was open and a junkie moved over and mumbled 'Give me a hand-out, buddy.' Ted foolishly stuck his hand through the window, but pulled it back in again pretty quickly when, in an attempt to lighten the atmosphere, I told him to count his fingers.

We began filming in an uneasy state of truce: the path carefully paved and the word out but, should the message have failed to filter through, six armed black policemen were stationed round the set and a squad of young Black Muslims in separate groups stood a few yards from the camera. The Muslims are purportedly to help with crowd control, but in fact are appointed by the precinct mosque for our protection.

The brooding atmosphere increased the unease among the

British members of the unit, who had been enlightened by last week's *Sunday Times* Magazine special on violence in New York. In the first nine months of 1972 there were 1,346 murders in the city: ten times the total for the whole of Britain. In the peak period there were fifty-eight killings in a week, fourteen in one day. The article was luridly illustrated with the mutilated bodies of murder victims in Harlem, their heads battered in by hammers; less violent but equally appalling were pictures of junkies dead from drugs stretched on tawdry mattresses in seedy Harlem hotels.

We rehearsed one of my fight scenes on 118th Street and I have never seen such staggering filth and garbage in one square block. The block beseeches demolition and, by the look of the charred black buildings and twisted fire escapes, someone has already made a bid to burn it down.

The fight scene is where Bond frees himself from his captors after a visit to Mr Big's Harlem hideout, the Fillet of Soul. It takes place in a derelict slum, but our real slum had to be cleaned up a bit before we could use it, so that Jimmy Bond could leap about without getting six-inch rusty nails and broken glass in his socks.

If the atmosphere was uncertain, so was the barometer. An odd thing about New York is the way the temperature topples within the hour by five to ten degrees. The morning began with beautiful sunshine and blue skies and by three in the afternoon it had turned into a grim, grey, freezing day and I was glad to sit between shots in the warm, comfortable caravan which the New York unit had provided.

Tonight we caught up with Fabergé's President, George Barrie, who had promised us a visit in Jamaica. George, his wife, Gloria, Luisa and I visited another of Frank Sinatra's haunts, Le Mistral, on 52nd Street. The last time we were there, so was he. It is one of New York's fine French restaurants and I was happy to see my old friend again, Jean Larriega, its French proprietor.

* * *

B-Day Seventy-eight. Eight o'clock in the morning and cumbrous banks of low grey cloud seem to rest on the tops of the skyscrapers. A jerky drive literally 'across 110th Street', which was the title of Yaphet Kotto's last movie about gang warfare and the street which marks the Harlem border.

Far along the faded end of Fifth Avenue the car stopped, where the crew had collected at the cross-section of 117th Street. There again was the grim granite of the block which was once adjudged the worst in New York City for crime, conditions, prostitution and poverty.

Today's scenes continue those we covered yesterday. Jimmy is being escorted from the back room of the Fillet of Soul after his first, and possibly his last, encounter with Mr Big. The back door we used opened onto a sleazy, littered alley which slices through the block. Jim is about to be disposed of by Mr Big's henchmen, but with a few quick kicks and some help from Harold Strutter of the CIA, he escapes.

The sudden flashing of fire-engine lights and the wail of sirens stopped our shooting and an old building burst into flames a block away. We watched while firemen fought a losing battle and then Cubby, who was standing by my side, noticed one of the policemen had an ash cross on his forehead commemorating Ash Wednesday, which is today.

Cubby told the patrolman he would like to go to church and asked where the nearest one was. The policeman pointed over to Lennox Avenue which flanks Fifth Avenue and said, 'There is one just there, but you had better take someone with you because you are likely to get mugged.'

Lunch today was something of a disaster. We all went to a nearby Black Muslim soul food restaurant with a mosque on the floor above. A rigid no-smoking, no-drinking rule was applied and unit members who lit up were told to put their cigarettes out. After tasting the food I felt it would have been better if they had allowed drinking and smoking,

177

but no eating, on the premises. The same building was petrol-bombed and burned out after the murder of Malcolm X by those who believed the Black Muslims had a hand in his death.

This is an area where white faces are seldom seen; where some policemen have hidden shoulder holsters as well as side guns, but where the casualty rate among them still increases. A few streets from our location while we have been here, a black policeman was shot dead by two white patrolmen. The dead man was off duty in plain clothes but gave chase to a man who had held up a store. The two white policemen picked up the call in their patrol car, then saw a man, gun in hand, running down the street. What happened after that is in dispute, but there is no doubt that the black policeman is dead. He was hit six times.

Tragically, the body of a twelve-year-old girl who had been missing for thirty-six hours, was found yesterday in a yard two blocks away. Last night an undercover narcotics agent survived a stabbing after he had approached two local pushers who had run out of drugs. They did not know who he was, but assumed he must have money and tried to mug him.

A bizarre cover for a numbers racket rendezvous which could have been the brainchild of our Mr Big was discovered three blocks west of here during the last twenty-four hours. After a patrolman noticed a man step out of a derelict butcher's shop the police raided the block, which is almost deserted, and found a labyrinth of hidden passages, trapdoors, a drawbridge and a way out through one of the windows which seemed to have been bricked up. A push from inside one of the windows, and the phoney brickwork swung open. The man who masterminds the numbers business for this area does it, they say locally, from jail. If that is what he does with brick walls, it is hardly surprising. Lon Satton, who plays Harold Strutter of the CIA, had a prophetic line of dialogue today. It was: 'We'd better get

178

out of this neighbourhood.' Guy has heard rumblings of resentment from a local group about our shooting there.

Returning from the Harlem location tonight we got stuck in a traffic jam a few hundred yards from the Warwick. Police were controlling a crowd which was demonstrating against Golda Meir, who was visiting the Hilton Hotel opposite. Later, while Luisa was taking pictures of me on our apartment terrace for the *Daily Mirror*, she leant over the wall with the camera in her hand. Policemen posted on the Hilton roof spun round and I pulled her back.

B-Day Seventy-nine. 007 was busy today tracking down a pimpmobile. To call these forty-thousand-dollar phantasmagorical status symbols 'cars' is to do them an injustice. They come in all colours and customized versions of anything from a Cadillac Eldorado to a Chevrolet Corvette. They are dubbed pimpmobiles by dazzled New Yorkers because some of the proud owners have made their pile in prostitution, protection and drug peddling in Harlem. Long, low caricatures of cars, their fronts are all grill and glitter and seem a sort of cross between a colossal chromium coffee machine and a cartoonist's Rolls-Royce. I would love to drive one down the byways near my home in Buckinghamshire, if only to watch the jaws drop in disbelief, but the thought of import duty on top of the purchase price dissuades me.

That Mr Big should own one is obligatory. Bond spies it outside a voodoo cult shop and when he sees Mr Big, Solitaire and Tee Hee driving off, he hails a taxi and follows them to Harlem. But the taxi driver is Mr Big's man; the same driver who later in the story picks him up outside New Orleans International Airport. We have, of course, already shot this scene in New Orleans and unfortunately Arnold Williams, the actor who played the part, got himself engaged on another production and was not available today, so we had to use a double. He must have been hired because he looks like Arnold and certainly not for his driving ability. The part called for him to drive up and stop at a marked spot on the road while I got in. This man could not have driven through Arsenal's goalposts on a sunny day. The first time he tried it he stopped yards from the mark and I had to leap across to open the door.

He let the clutch out so fiercely that, to the delight of a few locals, gathered to gape, I was thrown into a heap in the back. After about the twentieth take we managed to get something approaching what Guy actually wanted in the can before fading light put an end to the day's shooting.

As the light lowered in the Harlem street where we were finishing, a street a few blocks deeper into the quarter was lit by a bang and bursting flame. A empty pimpmobile, the epitome of some gentleman's success, was petrol-bombed by the kerbside. The owner was due to testify in a narcotics case the next day, and the gesture suggests that if he did he would be in the hot seat. Bombing a Harlem hoodlum's buggy is said to be the biggest insult in the book. No doubt he cried all the way to the junkyard.

Tonight David Tebet fixed us up with tickets for the hit Broadway musical *Pippin*, the new show from Stephen Schwartz, who wrote *Godspell*. It is one of the finest musicals of all time, beautifully staged and with brilliant performances. Bob Fosse, who directed *Cabaret*, was both director and choreographer. Driving up Broadway brought back memories for me of the night I starred in a Broadway show. It *was* only one night. With Joan Miller, I opened in *A Pin to See the Peepshow* on 17 September 1953 and closed on 17 September 1953. I was one of the last to know, as I didn't appear until the fourth scene and arrived at the theatre for the second night after the rest of the cast. Some-one pushed a piece of paper in my hand and I read: 'As from 17 September the show is closed.' Baffled, I said, 'But that was yesterday.' Then someone explained that by issuing notice on closure night the producers would save themselves a day's salary. I remember spending the rest of the evening at the movies clutching my case of unused make-up. Not a star overnight, but a one-night star.

B-Day Eighty began with a stand-by. Guy took pity on me and, as I wasn't needed in the first two shots, let me lie in bed a bit longer. But my subconscious time system still woke me up at 5.30 AM, despite a late-night carousing around town with Harry Belafonte.

The evening had begun with a champagne cocktail party on my behalf at Bollinger's Park Avenue headquarters for twenty-five out-of-town journalists, among them some familiar faces from New Orleans. Duty done, we arrived at Harry's apartment, to be greeted by his wife, Julie, and their children. I see Harry quite often, last time a year ago in London with Sidney Poitier, but I haven't seen the children for seven years, when we were all in Aruba together. What a shock it is when you realize the years are passing. David, then a tiny boy, is now fifteen and as devastatingly handsome as his father; his then four-year-old sister is now a ladylike eleven-year-old. Harry was finishing his latest album and arrived later in his blue Levi working clothes – rather like my Bond outfit, but it looked better on him. After his swift three-minute changing act he took us off to Jimmy's, the meeting place of the media where the higher echelons of political journalists gather to dissect affairs of state and the state of affairs. Harry said if you want to know the political score on someone, or their position in the market, just ask a question in Jimmy's and within twenty-four hours you will get your answer.

When the call came for me to get to work this morning it was to Second Avenue at 94th Street, but to the confusion of New Yorkers our Art Department had altered the street sign to read 124th Street, which is deep in Harlem. The corner had been spotted on a location recce and deemed perfect for the exterior of the Fillet of Soul restaurant, which the script locates in Harlem. Our Art Department considered it was easier to change the map of New York than find another corner.

Arnold Williams, the actor who played the taxi driver in New Orleans, joined us today, so I didn't have to put up with his double's driving. Trying to control the traffic so that Arnold could drive his taxi half a block up the road with me in the back was hysterical. Assistants ran in circles like circus ponies and Crackers kept calling on the two-way walkie-talkie radio for Arnold to get out in the middle of the road. New Yorkers, not noted for their patience, piled up behind us tooting their car horns and, mounting the pavement to pass, were soon snarled in a jumbo jam. We were rescued by a little old lady who marched to the middle of the road and took over traffic control. Waving her arms and bellowing, 'Hold it right there, buster,' and 'Move it, you mothers!', much to everyone's amusement, she soon had traffic trickling through to order. We managed to keep her out of camera range and she really was a great help.

David Tebet worked his magic and got more tickets for a Broadway show tonight for Cubby, his wife Dana, David Hedison, Luisa and me. This time they were for *A Little Night Music* with Glynis Johns and Hermione Gingold; after the show we paid a return visit to Le Mistral. The trouble with New York is not that my mornings start all too early, but that my nights finish all too late.

I will inter B-Day Eighty-one as best forgotten, in the underground garage below East 65th Street where we spent a stifling day shooting, creeping around and under parked cars, keeping an eye on Dr Kananga. With the heat from our arc lights in the unventilated, confined space, the crew and myself were not quite sure whether we were being cooked or buried alive.

The day ended on a sigh of relief. The rushes of our first day's filming in New York went astray on their way to London and have been bobbing about the globe for four days. Tracked to Istanbul, they have been returned to their proper place, the cutting rooms at Pinewood.

B for billion-dollar Bond Day Eighty-two. The most expensive drama Bond can ever encounter, taking full account of Tom Mankiewicz's fertile mind, is fact not fiction, and began with a mysterious phone call to the Fleming-like character of Charles Russhon late yesterday.

Charles, who soars above six feet, is Harry and Cubby's Mr Fixit in the United States. In General Wingate's Burma invasion Charles, a former USAAF colonel and Government Special Investigator, made the first night flight, without lights, in a glider filled with British troops. He has more medals than he wants to polish: the Purple Heart twice, the American DFC, the British DFC, the Presidential Citation, the Philippines Citation, the Silver Star, the Bronze Star, the Air Medal and the Major General's Commendation.

On *Live and Let Die* Charles fixed the charter flight we took from New Orleans to Jamaica inside twenty-four hours after the original arrangement fell through; he found the planes we smashed in New Orleans; and got quick US official clearance for the fourteen guns we took to Jamaica. He turned up such props as the Pulsar wrist computer which I wore, and his latest gadget is a portable telephone carried in an attaché case, which came in useful yesterday. Charles's phone buzzed, the bulb on the outside lit up – and so did Charlie's face when he heard the news.

A call from the First Division of the New York City Police via the Mayor's office had disclosed that the Central Certificate Service of the New York Stock Exchange moving 2·3 million bonds' worth, a staggering sixty-three billion dollars, from their old vaults in Broad Street to their new building in nearby Water Street, on a route which cut right across our shooting path.

The call said with masterly understatement that there could be 'a little conflict on the schedule'. That there could. With pimpmobiles crossing, Bond cars crashing across the path of their three armoured trucks and over one hundred specially assigned armed New York City Police and security men mingling with Mr Big's gun-toting black heavies.

Our shooting schedule could provide the perfect cover for the biggest hit in the history of the crime business, but it is impossible for the Central Certificate Service to delay their move because the bonds have to be on hand at the new headquarters when Wall Street goes back to work on Monday morning. We are also booked, or 'locked in', to other locations for the rest of our schedule here and a further day's shooting could cost from fifty to seventy-five thousand dollars. Charles and Steve Kesten, our Production Manager in New York, met the directors and Security Chief of the Central Certificate Service and did a deal.

With a small-scale switch in our shooting plan and a short diversion by the Certificate Service we would not even see each other. We both went ahead, and it worked. Although the surrounding streets were lined with police, there was no pile-up of pimpmobiles and armoured trucks.

In today's scenes Bond, just arrived from England, is met at the airport by Charlie, a CIA driver. They set off, Bond in the back seat, towards Manhattan. On the Franklin D. Roosevelt Drive a pimpmobile with Mr Big's henchman, Whisper, at the wheel, draws level. Whisper keeps his eyes on his dashboard; the speedometer slides back, revealing a camera viewfinder with two crosshairs meeting at the centre, where Charlie's head is visible. The crosshairs draw closer, the right rear-view mirror of the pimpmobile makes a half revolution, a hole opens in its side and a tiny, thin metal dart slams into Charlie's temple. As he slumps over the wheel

Bond dives over the front seat to get control of the car, but Charlie's foot is stuck on the throttle.

The car lurches wildly for the centre wall dividing the expressway, grazes it, bounces back into the stream of traffic and screams straight for a steel fence separating the road from an exit rampway. Bond succeeds in pushing the driver's inert body aside and, with a last-gasp effort, spins the wheel. The car bursts through the fence, over the pavement, hurtles up and down hotel steps and crashes into a fire hydrant. Bond emerges stirred and shaken but otherwise unharmed.

In the good old days this sort of thing was filmed on back projection with little likelihood of danger to life and limb, but that is not the way they do things on a Bond movie in 1973. There I was, screeching on two tyres at sixty miles an hour towards steel fences, tearing into traffic and bouncing off bumpers. My co-driver was Joie Chitwood, who masterminded our stunt driving in New Orleans. I think I know now how racing drivers and bullfighters, or anyone who dices with death for a living, feel when they face the moment of truth. Adrenalin pumps through your veins like a recharge; as Joie and I talked between takes he agreed that he got it too – and in fact couldn't work without it.

I experienced it first in Portugal at a farm where bulls were raised for the ring. An official guest, I was invited into a working arena where a bull was being put through its paces and the proceedings televised. My mouth felt dry and my knees weak as I walked to the centre of the ring, where a bullfighter handed me a cape and shouted incomprehensible Portuguese instructions, as the maddened animal pawed the ground and rolled its bloodshot eyes. For the first time I went on an adrenalin trip – a sort of undiluted courage injection which comes at times like these and helps you rise to the occasion.

I certainly needed the adrenalin today, and we must

spend another day tearing about in cars to complete the sequence; I cannot say I am looking forward to it.

The day was not without its drama for one of the other drivers, Al Gross, whose buggy was a red, resprayed Cadillac. Rehearsals and run-throughs had run him short of petrol so he set off to fill up the tank. Not a New Yorker, he became confused on the expressway and ended up cruising around Brooklyn, where two policemen pulled him up and began to grill him. The resprayed bodywork and the phoney licence plates of the Cadillac were evidence enough, but the walkie-talkie radio convinced them they had got one of a hot car ring currently operating in New York who are known to keep in contact with one another by radio. 'But I'm an actor in the James Bond movie,' protested Al, weakly.

'Oh, yeah,' said the Brooklyn cop, belligerently, 'and we're Clark Gable and Lana Turner.'

Al was saved by the timely crackle of the walkie-talkie; an assistant asked where the hell he was and told him to get his ass and car back to the location. Still not convinced, the cops escorted him back to FDR Drive, where he fell into Cubby's arms. Most of the unit had packed up to go home; five minutes later and we would have left – and he would have spent the night in jail.

B-Day Eighty-three: a day of depression. I arrived at Kennedy Airport, where we were to film Bond's arrival at the Pan Am Terminal, to be greeted by long faces from Guy and Cubby. They had good reason for despair. Film of three days' work, including shooting in Harlem and Saturday's expensive stunts, was at that moment being tested in a London laboratory with a worse-than-even chance that the film was ruined and the whole lot would have to be re-shot.

Harry's secretary, Sue Parker, carrying the rushes back to London, had been asked to open the canisters of film in a security check at Kennedy Airport, despite advance clearance by Customs. She refused to open them and explained that it would ruin the film. They were taken from her and put through the X-ray machine used to spot guns or bombs in baggage. The odds on undeveloped film going through an X-ray machine and coming out undamaged are low, and the first message was bad. By four o'clock we had moved to Central Park for some travelling shots and, after a miserably anxious day, the good news came. The film had been successfully screened in London.

Cubby took Guy, Ted Moore, Luisa and me to the '21' for a celebratory dinner. Stanley Schneider, the President of Columbia, was throwing a party at his United Nations Plaza home for Ross Hunter, whose *Lost Horizon* opens here tomorrow night. We missed Ross on his last trip to London because we were in New Orleans, and it was nice to meet up with him and another old and dear friend, Nancy Sinatra, Snr.

B-Day Eighty-four, and I have a sneaking suspicion Cubby and Harry are trying to slide out of paying me for the last week by having me eliminated on the FDR Drive expressway. We were back again today for more mobile mayhem continuing the sequence we began on Saturday. The words of Dr David Hinds, who told my fortune in Jamaica, about a car accident and my suffering brain damage, ran riot through my head all day. At least, I thought ruefully, it will be a well-detailed demise. The cameras were everywhere; to our right, to our left, behind us and on top of us. About the only place they weren't was up my rear end which, considering the hairy stunts we were doing, was just as well.

Freddy Goldberg, the Vice President in charge of publicity and advertising for United Artists, created a continuity problem for us by coming down on Saturday and riding in one of the cars. What he could not have known was that the car he chose is one into which Joie and I crash. He brought me some cigars, which he presented before the ride, I am glad to say, because if he had waited until after I wouldn't have got them! After a couple of runs in the bumped buggy, Freddy suddenly remembered he had urgent business uptown.

The next victim was John Bryson, our special photographer in New Orleans and Jamaica, who is now with us on a magazine assignment. He couldn't refuse, as he is making a name for himself as a toughie character actor in two Sam Peckinpah movies, *The Getaway* and *Pat Garret and Billy the Kid*.

Here was his chance to prove himself true to his screen form! With the New York City Police blocking the traffic from three exits, we began our first run. I was leaning over Joie's slumped body, grabbing for the wheel, and in a co-steering job we thumped into the car carrying Bryson. The two car fenders clanged together and locked; we swayed at sixty miles an hour in an unwilling waltz to a concerto of clashing metal and screaming tyres. Joie kept saying, 'Christ; we're hooked. Christ! We're hooked!' and all I could think of to say was 'Help!' We tore free after what seemed an age and shuddered to a stop. We had to do the run three times more before the General was satisfied.

At seven o'clock this evening the phone rang. It was Crackers, saying with qualifying caution learned from years in the picture business: 'All being equal, that is, if the rushes are okayed tomorrow afternoon from London, you are finished on the picture.'

This was it, then, the party was over. I felt a terrible sense of anti-climax. Feeling numb, I mixed myself a very stiff drink. My mood was dispelled by the arrival of Elliot Kastner and Tessa Kennedy, who came round with David Hedison and, very appropriately, Chaim Topol, for dinner at Patsy's. With Topol I had had my first meal on arriving in America for *Live and Let Die*. How fitting that I should have one of my last meals of the production with him, too.

Luisa and I are leaving for California; the Broccolis have kindly loaned us their house in Beverley Hills, Hollywood, where I have been asked to present the Oscar for 'Best Actor'. Without wishing to sound too partisan, I hope I hand it to my mate, Michael Caine, who is nominated for his performance in *Sleuth*.

Later Joan Collins and Ron Kass are bringing our children to join us at Leslie and Evie Bricusse's house in Acapulco, where I will recuperate from the rigours of Bond.

After jetting the bayous in boats, whizzing around in a wingless plane, courting bites by crocodiles and crashing cars, I will always wryly recall my last line in *Live and Let Die*. Delivered to the driver on the Franklin D. Roosevelt Drive expressway, it was: 'Easy, Charlie, let's get there in one piece.'

Give or take a tooth, I did.

Ian Fleming

Ian Fleming, one of the most accomplished of thriller writers . . . mercilessly readable.
'It is not really their stories . . . that give Mr Fleming's thrillers their highly individual quality; it is their delicious trimmings – the careful deployment of technical detail, the gleeful display of worldliness, the frequent and by any standard brilliant flashes of description'
– SUNDAY TIMES

LIVE AND LET DIE   30p
The chief protagonist is the giant American Negro, head of a Voodoo cult, Mr Big. A hard weapon of fear and death who had no known vices except women, whom he consumed in quantities. Soviet agent and a member of SMERSH.

MOONRAKER   30p
Is he a national hero out to save the universe? Or a diabolical fiend bent on destruction? The answer must be found before the zero hour – an hour that is rapidly drawing closer and closer – when Moonraker will be finished and ready for use.

Dick Francis